GF3

The Diaries of Parker Pasha

Also by HVF Winstone

Captain Shakespear*
Gertrude Bell*
The Illicit Adventure
Leachman: 'OC Desert'*

with Zahra Freeth:

Kuwait: Prospect and Reality
Explorers of Arabia

Editor, with Gerald de Gaury:

The Spirit of the East*
The Road to Kabul*

*also published by Quartet Books

H V F WINSTONE

The Diaries of Parker Pasha

War in the desert 1914–18 told from the secret diaries of
Colonel Alfred Chevallier Parker, nephew of Lord Kitchener,
Governor of Sinai, and military intelligence chief in the
Arab Revolt.

Quartet Books
London Melbourne New York

First published by Quartet Books Limited 1983
A member of the Namara Group
27/29 Goodge Street, London W1P 1FD

Copyright © 1983 by H. V. F. Winstone

British Library Cataloguing in Publication Data

Parker, Pasha
    The diaries of Parker Pasha
    1. World war, 1914–1918—Campaigns—Africa, North
    2. Military intelligence—Africa, North—History
    3. World war, 1914–1918—Secret service—
    Great Britain
    I. Title   II. Winstone, H. V. F.
    940.54'23   D766.82

    ISBN 0–7043–2392–3

Typeset by AKM Associates (UK) Ltd, Southall, London
Printed and bound in Great Britain by
Mackays of Chatham Limited, Kent

For Anne Edgerley,
his daughter

Contents

List of Illustrations

Acknowledgements

All the documentary material and photographs used in this book, unless otherwise attributed, are the property of Mrs Anne Edgerley and copyright is vested in her. I thank her for permission to use them. I would also like to express my gratitude to the librarians and staff of the Ministry of Defence Library; the Imperial War Museum, London; the India Office Library and Records (British Library); the Royal Society for Asian Affairs; and the Royal Geographical Society, for permission to use material which is acknowledged in text and notes. Also Dr Robin Birdwell and the Middle East Centre, Cambridge; Mr Zakki Ahmad, Miss Annice Bell, Mrs Ruth Mallas, Mr P. S. Turner, Mr John Tyson and Mrs D. St C. Chandler for valuable help.

- -*- Ottoman provincial boundaries
- -*- Sinai – Ottoman frontier 1906
- ▲ Fortified British posts
- ■ Positions of Turkish armies at dawn 1 February 1915
- ➔ Direction of Turkish attacks 1-12 February 1915

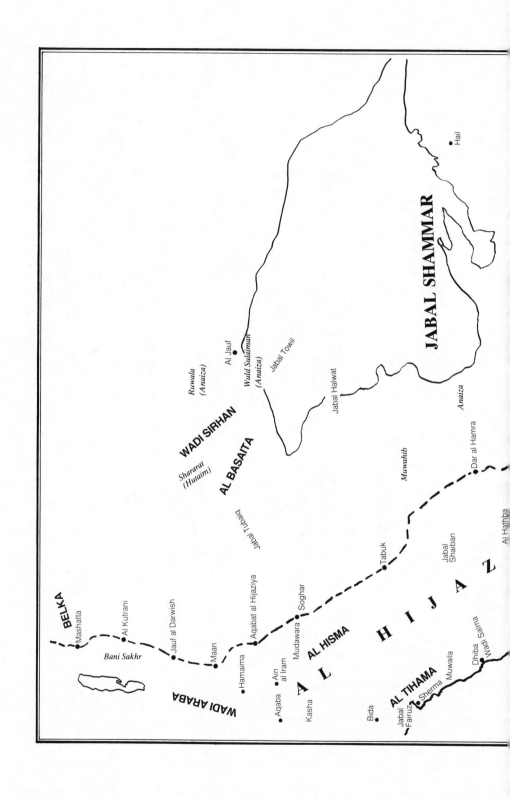

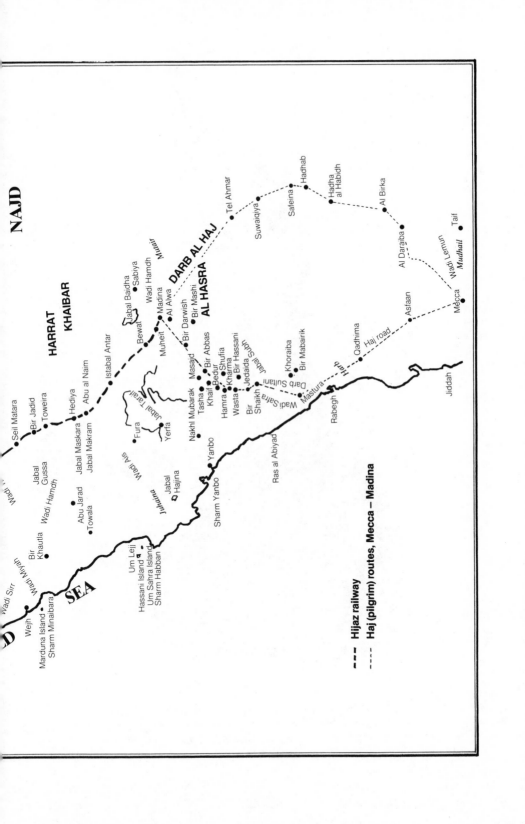

*Pilgrim banner, carried by generations of hajjis from Cairo
along the Sinai road to Maan, and thence to the holy cities of
the Hijaz. From Lady Anne Blunt's* A Pilgrimage to Najd, *published in 1881*

Introduction

Several years ago I decided to write the story of the Arab Bureau, that strange manifestation of political and military intelligence which grew out of Britain's Sharifian adventure during the First World War; a body whose place in history had been assured by the luminescent story told by its most famous son, T. E. Lawrence. My research for the book which came out of that resolve, *The Illicit Adventure*, led me to seek some of the other military and naval men who had been involved in the Arab Revolt, some serving the Bureau which was the hybrid child of Foreign Office and Army and Naval Intelligence, others working directly for the Expeditionary Force under Generals Maxwell, Murray and Allenby during the four years of the war. Some strange facts impressed themselves on me. Lawrence, who had brought the desert revolt to prominence in his *Seven Pillars of Wisdom*, had told a rattling tale, and the world had been duly mesmerized by it. His version of the story had been praised, and occasionally questioned, by a legion of commentators, ranging from military experts like Liddell Hart to writers such as Richard Aldington, subjected to flattery, to awe-inspired approbation and admiration, to psychoanalytical investigation and inventive re-telling. Writer and subject had attracted biographers and military experts all over the world. Yet, apart from a distinguished study of Allenby, the architect of victory, none of the generals involved had inspired a single study. And what of the other, lesser officers who had played vital roles in the desert war? What of Vickery who led the only observed campaign against the Turks in the Hijaz war, of Garland, the explosives expert and Ross the pilot whose stirring deeds were complemented by their mastery of Arabic, of Newcombe whose heroic deeds at Beersheba resulted in his capture and imprisonment? The list is long, yet nothing was known about such men. Nobody had even attempted to write their stories, to track them down when the war was over, or to seek their views. Aldington asked 'Why?' but nobody replied. Most of all, what of Col. Parker, chief of intelligence in Sinai from the outset, with Newcombe the senior staff officer at Intelligence HQ under the DMI, Brig.-Gen. Clayton, and the officer responsible for intelligence in the Hijaz when Lawrence went down to join the Sharif's sons?

I made my first task the running to earth of Col. Parker's surviving relatives, for I knew that he had died in retirement in 1935. It turned out to be a writer's nightmare.

The official registry was no help, for though the Colonel's last will and testament named his family home at Minchinhampton, and his wife as the chief beneficiary, there was no indication of the whereabouts of his son and daughter, and the family home had been sold. People in Minchinhampton, the beautiful Cotswold village to which my subject had retired in 1925, remembered the family only vaguely though they were able to point out the house, 'Westfield', on the common where they had lived. A ray of hope was offered by a lady of the place who remembered that the Colonel's daughter had qualified as an architect sometime before the Second World War and thought that she had married, but there was no clue to her husband's name. Finally, I tried the Royal Institute of British Architects, on the theory that not very many women would have qualified in the 1930s. They were able to tell me that Miss Parker was on their register and that she had become Mrs. Edgerley, the wife of a barrister. Thus I was eventually able to trace her.

Mrs. Edgerley had inherited a locked box from her father which contained a unique collection of documents, written and photographic. A methodical man, Parker had kept a personal note of all his secret activities throughout the war, including a diary of the first critical year of the Arab Revolt when he was the senior staff officer in the territory of the Sharif of Mecca, the Hijaz. It contained copies of intelligence telegrams and reports to and from GHQ, and a record of his activities in Sinai during the first Turkish assault on the Suez Canal in 1915.

Col. Parker seldom discussed his wartime activities with friends or family, and the military adventure which came to be known as the Arab Revolt was of no consuming interest to his children whose professional lives and intellectual pursuits lay in other directions. But they were of great concern to me. Mrs. Edgerley unhesitatingly placed the documents at my disposal when I was writing my earlier book, but unfortunately I could not make full use of her father's papers in that context.

It was a matter of some surprise to me that not one of the hundreds of scholars, writers and military historians who have written about Lawrence and the Sharifian affair over a period of more than fifty years had ever tried to contact Col. Parker in his lifetime, or to seek his papers after his death. Official records showed quite clearly that he was the first executive head of the Arab Bureau – though he quickly disposed of the role – and therefore the first chief of that erudite, self-motivated band in Cairo which included Dr D. G. Hogarth, Gertrude Bell, T. E. Lawrence, George Lloyd, and Aubrey Herbert. But they had not tried to contact other significant personalities either. All were, and remain, submerged by the pervasive legend of 'Lawrence of Arabia'. I hope that I may have contributed a little towards redressing the balance.

Brief explanations are called for of two matters of detail. Col. Parker's middle name, given throughout this work as 'Chevallier' derives from a collateral branch of the family, but at some stage one 'l' was dropped and my subject's birth certificate shows 'Chevalier'. However, almost all official and unofficial documents use the double consonant, and even within the family that usage persisted. I have therefore retained the common if incorrect spelling for the sake of consistency.

Consistency is impossible in another respect – Arabic

transliteration. In the case of place names I have tried to follow accepted practice, even where it is illogical to do so. Thus, many places beginning with 'K' should properly take a 'Q', such as Kasim and Kossaima; while the vowel sound represented by the Arabic 'y' in the middle of a word is variously represented as 'ay', 'ey', 'ai' in maps and books. Beersheba should be represented as *Bir al Saba* in logic, and Bethlehem as *Bait al Lahm.* Amir, Emir, even Ameer; Shaikh, Shaykh, Sheykh and Shayook. I have simply followed my instinct. I claim no particular justification.

H. V. F. Winstone, 1983

1
Baptism in Sinai

To the Arabs who occupied the bleak land between Suez and the southern desert of Palestine, Arabia Petraea, it was Tor.[1] To the rest of the world it was Sinai, and its overlord in the years immediately after the war of 1914–18 was the Englishman, Alfred Chevallier Parker.

It was perhaps appropriate that Parker should be sent to that god-forsaken waste in 1906. It was the year of allied war plans. The year in which war threatened in reality, as a Turkish force occupied Aqaba and Britain demanded its withdrawal at sword-point. Parker was, after all, the nephew of England's most illustrious soldier, Horatio Herbert Field Marshal Lord Kitchener of Khartoum, victor of Omdurman and South Africa, C-in-C India, the favourite son of king and people.

Kitchener had skirted the same lands in his youth, mapping the Wilderness of Zin and the routes of the tribes and of Moses's spies with his friend Claude Conder of the same regiment, the REs, in the name of the Palestine Exploration Fund.

The omens for a British governor and his small garrison in the remote, austere oasis of Nakhl were not good. The tribes of Tor were as deeply immersed in Hamitic superstition and tribal fanaticism as their forefathers had been centuries before when Moses led the tribes of Israel down to the Sea of Reeds and across the parted waters to Elim and Rephidim and the mountains of

Tih and on to Ezion-Geber and the Land of the Philistines. Ownership of the desolate peninsula remained a matter of doubt, for Britain ruled it in 1906 with the same uncertain title by which she laid claim to Egypt. 'Sinai is part of Egypt', Cromer had declared after the occupation of Egypt in 1882. But Egypt and Sinai had belonged to the Ottoman Turks for four centuries when Britain took over the territory, and in all that time only the north-west segment had formed part of Egypt, marked off by a line from Suez to Rafa on the coast, just west of Gaza in the Ottoman Sanjak of Jerusalem. Cromer had insisted on a line from Rafa to Aqaba, which was Ezion-Geber, and announced in his unequivocal way: 'That is the eastern boundary of Egypt.'[2]

At best it was an equivocal boundary, but Britain's governor would defend it resolutely while keeping the peace with the old ally Turkey, whose army paraded on its perimeter, and with the tribes which roamed its infertile interior.

Capt. Parker was thirty-two when he arrived to take up his post. Tall, almost gaunt of face with a quiet manner, he had already proved himself on the North-West Frontier (medal and two clasps at Tirah) and in the Sudan with Kitchener's army. His names betrayed the family connection. Otherwise few of his fellow officers or even his personal friends ever knew that he was Kitchener's nephew. He was not a man to seek favours; and certainly he would have resisted any suggestion of nepotism, though preferment through family connections was not uncommon in the army of his day.

His paternal grandfather was Sir James Parker, a vice-chancellor of England, who married Mary Babington of Rothley Temple, the Leicestershire hall of the Knights Templars. Sir James died from heart trouble at forty-two. His son, Henry, married Frances Emily Kitchener, the eldest daughter of Lieut.-Col. Henry Horatio Kitchener (13th Light Dragoons and 9th and 29th Foot, born two days before the Battle of Trafalgar), and Frances Ann (daughter by his third wife of the Revd. John Chevallier of Aspall Hall, Suffolk). Henry Horatio Kitchener sold his commission in 1849 and took the family to Ireland in the wake of the great potato famine. In 1850 Horatio Herbert was

born. It is recorded that if the very different children of the family
had one thing in common it was an adoration of their mother
Frances, who died at Montreaux in 1864. Two years after her
death Col. Kitchener married Emma Green, daughter Frances
Emily's New Zealand born music teacher.

Frances Emily, who was always known as 'Millie', was the
antithesis of her shy, taciturn brother. She smoked cigars, was
perhaps the first woman ever to ride in a horserace, and was an
exceptionally good shot or – as she would insist – 'marksman'. It
was a family of opposites, indeed, in which strong and extrovert
women appear to have reduced most of the menfolk to a
comparatively silent fortitude in marriage. Henry Parker, her
pleasant, easy-going husband, had an eye put out by an arrow at
Harrow school, but for almost the whole of his life refused to
name the culprit. At the end it was revealed that a cousin had done
the deed.

Financial problems eventually forced Henry Parker to sell
Rothley Temple, and he and Millie emigrated to New Zealand
where Alfred Chevallier was born. He was sent back to prep
school, of which his only recollection in later years was that he
seemed to be the only commoner among its intake. He went on to
his father's old school, Harrow, where his fees were paid by cousin
Alfred. He became known during his schooldays as 'Wallier'
(with a short 'a'). Nobody ever knew why, but the name was to
stick throughout his life. He was in Grove House along with two
Trevelyans, a Wolfe-Murray, George du Maurier, and others
whose reputations would shine in future years; but his own years
at that famous school, 1887–91, were unmarked by any
distinction save the winning of a 'carrying race' with G. E. W.
Hood in 1890.

On 13 April 1891, Col. Henry Kitchener wrote to his daughter
Millie about her son's future, a letter which throws interesting
light on his own son's future attitudes, not least his alleged
antipathy to the opposite sex.

My dear Millie
    I want to write to you about Wallier, who came here on his way to

THE GROVE.

E. E. BOWEN'S, ESQ., HOUSE.

SEPTEMBER, 1889.

M.	C. G. Pope**△¶	R. (a.)	G. M. Trevelyan
	F. W. Stephenson¶	M.R.	H. R. Dixon
VI. 1.	R. C. Trevelyan††		R. W. Bradley
M. VI.	A. Hardcastle‖	S. 1.	E. F. Usborne
VI. 1.	J. E. Sandilands§	M.S. 1.	Hon. W. Strutt
VI. 2.	F. L. D. Elliott		K. W. F. Edgecumbe§‡
V. 2.	T. M. Booth		F. W. Richey
	G. O. Scorer§		C. S. Rome
	J. H. Parker	S. 2.	A. Wormald†
	H. S. Sanderson*†=	M.S. 2.	E. C. Kitson
	H. D. Kendal-Grimston		R. M. Laird
M.V. 2.	H. A. L. H. Wade	S. 3.	H. F. Stirling
	H. B. Farquhar		J. P. Bagwell
	G. S. Clive	M.S. 3.	A. L. Moulton-Barrett
V. 3.	A. L. Tregoning		S. F. Watson
	G. E. W. Hood	IV. 1.	H. R. Yorke
	G. H. E. B. du Maurier	IV. 2.	G. Wolfe-Murray
M.V. 3.	J. W. Sandilands	IV.3.(a.)	F. Pope
R. (a.)	C. N. Irven		H. Edmeades
	R. B. Sheridan	IV.3.(b.)	J. Collinge
	A. C. Parker		B. F. S. W. Pinney
	A. F. Harrison*		

* House Cricket Eleven.   § House Gymnasium Four.
† House Football Eleven.   ‡ School Gymnasium Eight.
= House Fives Player.   △ School Cricket Eleven.
‖ House Racquet Player.   ¶ Philathletic Club.

J. C. WILBEE, PRINTER, HARROW.

Harrow School House List, 1889

Scotland. . . . I thought he was rather depressed but the party in the oak room said he was not and he worked away at the trees as usual. George Parker came yesterday and we talked about Wallier's going to Sandhurst not Woolwich. He told me that Bowen (House master) had told him that Wallier was above average as to intellect and that he was anything but an idle boy, but he said that he could not be got up sufficiently in mathematics to pass for Woolwich. . . . But that Sandhurst was exceedingly easy for him. I must remark upon this that I presume Woolwich would have given trouble and Sandhurst didn't. I think it was the College not Wallier. Now according to my experience I hope I shall show you that Wallier is quite as well at Sandhurst as at Woolwich and the reasons that make many parents prefer it to Woolwich. 1st it's a year longer at Woolwich, expense to the parent and drudgery to the boy. 2nd If he gets into the Engineers and does not, as Herbert did, get out of it which very few do, his duties are not over-pleasant, he is very much by himself and if with other officers they are *generally* married. The consequence of their being so often separated from other people. Moreover I do not think they are as a rule acceptable to the other branches of the service. . . . If he gets into the Artillery their messes are frequently very small and they often marry in consequence. They however can look forward if smart and with a good income to the Jacket of the Horse Artillery. For this many who could have [been] Engineers take Artillery in preference. Should he go to Sandhurst he will be able to choose whether he goes with Cavalry or the Guards, the Infantry or the India service. He will never have the marriage dangers and he will have the same opportunities of getting forward as many good men have before him. I may be wrong, for I did not speak to Wallier about it, but I fancy he would be happier did he know that you and Harry [Henry] would be satisfied as to Sandhurst. I feel I ought to write this to you and you must take it for what it is worth. . . . Tub will be with you ere this who will have told you all our news.

Yours affectionately,

H. H. Kitchener

Brother 'Tub', James Herbert Parker, who was at Harrow with Wallier, was destined to die in the Boer War. Wallier went to Sandhurst despite the apparent misgivings of Millie, and left on

Conington
Leicester.
April 13th 1891.

My dear Millie.

I want to write to you about Walter, who came here on his way to Scotland — On taking his arm I thought it was all bone but I believe it was only as usual. I thought he was rather depressed but the party in the Oak room said he was not & he worked away at the trees as usual. George Parker came yesterday & we talked about Walter's going to Sandhurst not Woolwich — He told me that Bowen had told him that Walter was above the average as to intellect & that he was anything but an idle boy, but he said that he could not be got up sufficiently in mathematics to pass for Woolwich. That their coaches could not get him up. But that Sandhurst was exceedingly easy for him — I

Colonel H. H. Kitchener's letter to his daughter Millie, Parker's mother, April 1891

the unattached list, going home to New Zealand where he joined the Colonial army before returning to England and a commission in the Royal Sussex Regiment in 1895. He soon saw service on the North-West Frontier, an experience which was to win him his first campaign medals and to prevent him from serving in South Africa, for the Indian High Command, with its own domestic problems at the time, could not spare its own men or the British regiments serving in the sub-continent for the conflict in which uncle Herbert was to add to the lustre of Omdurman.

If he was to be known to family and fellow soldiers throughout his life as 'Wallier', Parker would acquire another name among the Arabs of Sinai. Having no 'P' in their alphabet, and no ending such as the English 'er', they called him Birkil (or Barkal in some transliterations) and sometimes they used the courtesy title 'Beq', or as the British would have it 'Bey'. In the course of time the Khedive of Egypt would upgrade the title to the lordly Basha, or as it is in English, 'Pasha'.

He went to Egypt in 1899 fresh from novitiate service as a subaltern in India, and was taken into the Intelligence Department in 1901 under Major the Count Gleichen. In 1905 he was appointed deputy Director of Military Intelligence in Cairo, then under the control of Maj. R. C. R. Owen who was shortly to be succeeded by Col. Lee Oliver Stack.

On 6 May 1906, as trouble brewed in Sinai, Owen sent him written instructions, addressed formally to 'Al Kaimakam A. C. Parker, Assistant Director of Intelligence':

You will proceed to Al Arish via Kantara by the 6.15 p.m. train this evening, and on arrival there you will take over the duties of Acting Governor. You will administer the whole of the Al Arish District and you must understand that all routine work connected with the Ministry of the Interior should go on as usual. The Turks have encroached on Egyptian territory near RAFA and have pulled down the boundary pillars near there and substituted a certain number of Egyptian pattern Telegraph poles for those of Turkish pattern. You should send out constant and frequent patrols in the direction of Rafa, and also employ a certain number of local and reliable Arabs to give you early information of any advance of the Turks. You should immediately report any such advance by telegraph to me. You should try and obtain information as to whether the Turks are collecting or emassing in the vicinity of Rafa or Gaza, preparatory to an advance, stating if possible the composition of their force. You should endeavour to ascertain the attitude of the local population and Arabs. I am sending with you Mulazim Awal Mikhail Effendi Habib, the Nazir of Nakhl. You will find him very useful in assisting you to keep in touch with Natives. You will find at Kantara 23 ME Carbines and 2,300 rounds of ammunition, which you will take with you to Al Arish and re-arm the 23 Sudanese Police whom you will find there. You will probably find many cases of complaints by the Arabs of ill treatment by the Turks – you should make a full enquiry into their complaints, and report. You are authorized to spend up to £50 on Secret Service. Should you require more, you should telegraph for authority. Should the Turks advance, you will not evacuate and retire from the fort unless attacked by a very superior Force, or unless you have very reliable information that a large force is advancing. You should ascertain as soon as possible how many of the Natives are armed, and what show of force you could make together with them against the Turks. If you find you have to retire from Al Arish, you must destroy the Telegraph apparatus before you leave.

R. C. R. Owen, Director of Intelligence, War Office, Cairo

An emergency appointment made in the face of a largely illusory threat was to last for six years, in which time Parker was to win the affection and loyalty of the Sinai tribes to the point where he was kept in his remote and lonely governorship by popular demand, despite his protestations to the War Office that his army career had been jeopardized by what was, in effect, a job for a civil servant.

Other Europeans before him had moved with mixed feelings among the wild tribes of the peninsula. Some time before the birth of Christ, a warrior had carved his feelings on a rock in the universal manner of the aggrieved:

'An evil race! I Lupus, a soldier, wrote this with my own hand.'[3]

Some visitors to Sinai came without illusion, others with a romantic vision of the Arab of the desert. Most came for, or under the guise of, the Queen's favourite charity, the Exploration Fund, to retrace the footsteps of the biblical invaders, and perhaps to keep an eye on other contemporary travellers as they sought the ancient route to the Mount of Moses and beyond.

A few entered the peninsula from southern Palestine and Midian, the stony, lava-strewn wasteland of Arabia Petraea, to search for copper-veins, manganese and even gold among the mountains of the Red Sea and in the deserts of the biblical tribes.

Sir Francis Henniker, Sir Richard Burton, Greville Chester, Capt. Charles Wilson of the REs who preceded Kitchener and Conder on behalf of Sir Henry James's Ordnance Survey – none who came before Parker had taken the peoples of these wastelands so much into his affections as the bohemian Henry Palmer, Lord Almoner's Professor of Arabic in the University of Cambridge.

After fourteen years of wandering in biblical and arch-aeological tracks he returned in 1882 with one of the finest of Britain's intelligence officers, William Gill, and a young naval officer from a family distinguished as brewers of beer, Lieut. John Charrington. Palmer, the wildly eccentric Arabist who was the friend of the world's wandering peoples, the gypsies of Europe and the Bedouin of the desert, who spoke Romany and Arabic with native fluency, translated the New Testament into Farsi, and wrote leading articles for *The Times*, was sent to Sinai in the vanguard of the Egyptian Expeditionary Force to prepare the way for Lord Wolseley's army by bribing the tribes to neutrality or to fight on Britain's side. The brave, resourceful Gill, who had played the Great Game courageously in central Asia, would cut the telegraph which kept Egyptian revolutionaries in touch with their masters in Constantinople.

The three men – Charrington was there to give added strength to the party – were lured into the confidence of tribesmen whom Palmer trusted as his own family, led to a cliff top on the lonely pilgrim road from Suez to Aqaba – the road which skirted the governor's residence at Nakhl – and shot in the back and hurled over the edge. Palmer had carried £3,000 in gold sovereigns with which to pay off the tribal shaikhs. The bodies of the three Englishmen were mutilated beyond recognition and, needless to say, the money was never seen again.

The fortress of Nakhl then was occupied by an Eyptian governor, one of four men who ruled Sinai on behalf of the Khedive of Cairo from the forts of Suez, Al Arish, Nakhl and Aqaba. Usually the men chosen for the job were ruffians who had served prison sentences. They were deemed the most suitable candidates to deal with the wild men and to endure the heat and unrelieved boredom of Sinai. They plotted as a matter of habit against their sovereign and worked for anyone who made it worth their while. In 1882 they were in league with the nationalist saviour Ahmad Arabi.

Most of the culprits had been found and hanged in the intervening years, but a few were still at large when Capt. Parker arrived twenty-four years later to take over the governor's seat at Nakhl.[4] This had remained vacant since its Egyptian occupant went to prison for plotting the murder of the three Englishmen.

The Gulfs of Suez and Aqaba emerge from the Red Sea like a victory sign. At their uppermost tips they are joined by an ancient road which runs across scorched sand and wind-flayed rock, as if to make an equilateral triangle of the peninsula and mark it off from the adjoining land masses of Africa and Asia Minor. It is the pilgrim road, worn deep by the tread of the faithful of a thousand years and more as they made the annual Haj journey from Cairo to Mecca. It joins the Haj road from Damascus about 50 miles north-east of Aqaba. Another track, made by the trade caravans of ages past, runs from Suez to Al Arish on the Mediterranean coast. Almost exactly half way along the Suez–Aqaba road is the fortress of Kalat Nakhl, which, like its sister watch towers in the remote regions of the Ottoman Empire, monitored for nearly five centuries the passage of armies and spies, one way and the other. In the care of the Egyptian Vice-Regent Muhammad Ali, who usurped the authority of his master the Sultan of Turkey in 1805, and of his family successors, the citadels of Sinai fell into ruins, serving only as places to which the desert shaikhs could be summoned for reprimand or proposition. The nineteenth-century view of the northern region was set down on paper by Greville Chester who visited Al Arish in 1880:

The town, or rather village of clay-houses, stands between the desert and the sea . . . It is dominated by a dilapidated fortress erected by Sultan Selim. To the west of the entrance of the Wady, close to the sea-shore, and near a Wely,[5] called Nabi Jasar, are the remains of some ancient house, one of which shows a ground plan of no fewer than seventeen rooms. Occasionally in winter, when heavy rains have fallen amongst the mountains inland, the Wady of Al Arish (the 'River of Egypt') is temporarily a turbulent, rushing torrent, but . . . during the rest of the year, it is a wide, dry Fiumara. Al Arish, or rather the Wadi of that place, is the natural boundary of Egypt, and appears as such in many maps. It is not, however, the political boundary between the Turkish Empire and vice-realm of Egypt. That is a day's journey farther on towards Gaza, at a place called Rafa, the ancient Raphia, where two ancient pillars have been re-erected as a landmark to the left of the track out of Egypt into Syria.[6]

Palmer himself described Nakhl: 'a wretched square fort in the midst of a glaring desert plain, the picture being backed up with some rather pretty limestone mountains'. In 1869 Palmer drank coffee there with the Nazir or Egyptian police chief, and they smoked their pipes on the great divan at one end of the barely furnished, austere hall. 'None of the soldiers were in uniform and they were as scoundrelly a set as one could well conceive.'[7]

The fortress of Aqaba was the most businesslike. The Frenchman Laborde described it in 1829:

It is at present, externally at least, in a sufficiently good state to resist the inroads of the neighbouring tribes, who, though not deficient in courage, have no means for enabling them to assail it with success . . . The governor has taken to himself the south-western bastion . . . The gunner, who is the military chief, inhabits the bastion to the south-east, and, like a veteran military man, sleeps by the side of a cannon. This gun, a twelve-pounder, and another which is planted in the north-eastern tower, are the only pieces capable of being discharged in case of an attack – an event however, of which happily there is little danger.

The gunner, it seemed, had added more peaceable pursuits to his official duties. He had converted a ruined mosque into a thriving trade warehouse. The fort was surrounded by a few miserable mud houses occupied by Arabs who lived by selling provisions to the garrison, and the tombs of warriors and pilgrims who had fallen by the wayside. The hills of Jabal Aqaba descended to the walls of the fort on its east side.

These places, and the little Christian village of Tor in the far south, were the only 'foreign' settlements of the peninsula, srrounded like the old Roman outposts in Britain and Syria by hostile tribes. In general, the Egyptian soldiers and governors who occupied them were ruffians, sent to expiate crimes, to hide from their fellow men habits and diseases too deplorable for urban society to accommodate.

Of the tribes themselves, most are descendants of the Bani Atiya of Arabia and the Maaza of Egypt. In the far south of the peninsula, the Muzeina, a noble tribe from the Arabian Hijaz, dominated in the nineteenth century. The great central plain of Tih was occupied by the Tiyaha who lived by supplying camels to pilgrims on the Suez-Aqaba road, and by guiding travellers in uncharted desert regions; occasionally they plundered the powerful Anaiza tribes as far north as Tadmor (Palmyra), returning with hordes of stolen camels. Their neighbours to the north and east were the Terabin whose territory stretched from the Wadi Arish to Gaza and the Dead Sea in Palestine. From Suez to Mount Sinai ran the writ of the Howaitat, swarthy and aggressive, stretching their territorial gains by constant wars with fellow Badu. According to their version of history, the human race was originally divided into three: the tent-makers, the agriculturalists, and the Howaitat. It has been suggested that in their view the first two classes were created entirely for the support of the third. The Howaitat are distinguished from all other Arabs of the desert by their bright

Kitcheners and Parkers, about 1870. L to R: Mrs Kitchener, Harry
R. Parker, Col. H.H. Kitchener, Frances Emily Kitchener ('Millie').
Girl on far right unidentified.

The Parkers of Rothley Temple. The young Wallier is second from right between father Harry and mother Millie. Cousin 'Tub' is on the far left, and sister Frances second from left.

Portrait of Millie, Lord Kitchener's sister and Parker's mother.

Alfred Chevallier 'Wallier' Parker, age about five.

At Harrow, age fourteen.

Subaltern, 1895.

Young officer in the Punjab.

Director of the Police School, Abbassiya, Cairo, 1912–14

Parker Pasha, Governor of the Frontier Provinces, 1924.

indigo-dyed *thobs*, their warlike qualities and their beautiful (often unveiled) women.[8] The true tribal *dira* is ancient Midian, between the Gulf of Aqaba and the northern Hijaz, but they also contested the territory east of the Jordan with the Bani Sakhr. The Howaitat laid claim to a large area east of Suez, and to country south of the Suez–Cairo road in Egypt. On the south-east border of the Tiyaha terrority camped the Lahaiwat tribe which came originally from central Arabia. That tribe also boasted a breakaway group consisting of about 250 families in 1906, just north of Suez, using the adopted name of Safaiha. It was a shaikh of that tribe who betrayed Professor Palmer and his companions in 1882, while the Howaitat and Lahaiwat tribes furnished the actual murderers.

Of the other tribes which Parker would come to know, perhaps the most important was the Aleiqat whose men claimed descent from an ancient people, the Bani Uqba, and who camped along the Gulf of Suez. All the tribes of the south were known as the Towara, Arabs of Tor; a motley assortment of Aleiqat, Jabeliya (mountain folk), Muzeina, and Sawalha. They were the guardians of the sacred mountain of the Prophet Musa; the recipients of free bread distributed twice daily by the monks of St Catherine, whose chapel crowned the summit.[9]

From the top of Mount Sinai it was possible to look across 200 miles of Egypt to the Shayib range along the Nile, and northward to Jabal Ejma. From there the hills of Hilal could be spotted, and from Hilal the pilgrim and the spy could look east to the green hills of Hebron, as did Joshua and Caleb as they plotted the way to the Promised Land. They were the sightings which gave Capt Parker his first panoramic views of Sinai and Arabia Petraea, as the Turks withdrew at gun-point from Aqaba and Britain kept up its vigil over lands to which it had, at best, a suffragan title.

Parker quickly came to close quarters with the tribes and their chiefs, especially with the children. It was hard to resist the children of Sinai, the ragged, scantily clothed infants who roamed the wilds and were sent out almost as soon as they could speak to tend the flocks of sheep and goats. Sometimes when camping out with his Sudanese guards he would find a child of the desert asleep at night amid a sheltering flock of sheep, protecting itself from the bitter cold.

Parker and his colleagues were carefully chosen for their task of maintaining law and order in Sinai: young men with experience of of desert warfare, good at picking up the languages and dialects of the tribes they moved among: strong and resolute, as they needed to be, for the tribes they came to govern in Sinai had never acknowledged the authority or desirability of government of any kind. Among the first to join him were the brothers Alwyn and 'Wiffy' Jennings Bramly and Capt. G. W. Murray. All were staff officers answerable through Parker to the Directorate of Military Intelligence in Cairo, and reporting through the DMI to the Austrian aristocrat who was Britain's Inspector-General, the chief of all intelligence civil and military, Maj.-Gen. Von Slatin.

Between them the new men built up their own intelligence network. Children, as is the custom in foreign 'news' gathering, were the best source of information. They were easily trained to turn up at appointed times and places. A few pennies placed in their grubby palms was handsome payment for the tit-bits of gossip and news which they innocently passed over.

Already German interest in the Middle East, which had steadily built up from the moment of the Kaiser's promise to support and protect Islam delivered at the tomb of Saleh-ad-Din in Damascus in 1898, threatened to oust Britain from its traditional strongholds. German pilgrims began to make their way in increasing numbers along the Sinai paths which led to the mount of Moses. Overtures had been made to tribal shaikhs, and to the monks of the Monastery of St Catherine. But Parker and his friend Alwyn Jennings Bramly, whom he made Inspector of the southern region of Tor, were a step ahead of the Germans, whose efforts were directed from Cairo by the Kaiser's Jewish friend Baron Max von Oppenheim, known to his British counterparts as 'The Spy'. One of the clerics of the mountain which was sacred to Jews, Christians and Muslims alike was the French theologian and epigraphist, Father Jaussen. And Father Jaussen, with his eye for detail and his protective religious habit, was the perfect intelligence agent. Parker lost no time in enlisting his services.

The need for reliable agents grew more urgent as the months went by from the summer of 1906. German incursions became alarming.

No less alarming were the revolutions of Persia and Turkey in 1906 and 1908 which brought in their wake a revitalized Arab and Persian sense of nationality, and a more sinister sense of empire on the part of Muslims the world over. Pan-Arabism and Pan-Islamism became important terms in the intelligence vocabulary of Europe. While Capt. Parker and his companions worked to win over the tribes of Sinai and brought the monks of St Catherine's into their network – they were to prove the most reliable of his spies in the peninsula when the moment of crisis came – their fellow staff-officers in Palestine and Syria, Persia and the Gulf, joined the fray.

A secret war began, a war designed to separate potential friend from potential foe in eastern territories which stretched from African Tripoli to Afghanistan and the North-West Frontier of India; from Tibet to Indonesia.

As military governor of Sinai and an officer of staff intelligence at Cairo, Parker was destined to play an important part in the struggle of the European powers for ascendancy in the region then known as the 'Near East'.

He remained at the Governor's residence, the austere fortress of Nakhl, until 1913, civilizing it with a flourishing garden and a squash court. Police posts were established there and at Arish, Kuntilla (the crossing point on the road which leads by Wadi Araba and Wadi Sirhan to the north Arabian nafud desert) and Aqaba. A network of British 'newsagents' was established to counter the Turkish espionage system with which the Young Turks of Constantinople had replaced the agents of the old 'Fox', Sultan Abdal Hamid. Parker had made the 'terrible wilderness' as secure as it could be in the shadow of a Turco-German *entente*. He established a well-trained and loyal Camel Corps to help maintain law and order among the unruly Bedouin. He had taken time off from the arduous task of governing the sons of Ishmael in 1910 to negotiate with the Jewish financial wizard at the Sublime Porte, Djavid Bey. He had talks too with Herr von Stamm the

German counsellor to the Berlin–Baghdad rail scheme.

By 1911 his uncle Lord Kitchener had taken over from the desperately sick Eldon Gorst, Cromer's successor, as Resident and Consul-General in Egypt. And the most thorough professional among Britain's military intelligence personnel, Maj.-Gen. Henry Wilson, took over the army wing of the secret service as Director of Military Operations.

In 1909 Parker married his second cousin, Winifred Margaret Parker, while on leave, at the established Church of Scotland at Fairlie in Ayrshire. His bride proved no exception to the dominance of the distaff established by the Kitchener ladies. She was the eldest daughter of Alfred Parker, his father's first cousin, the relative who had paid his school fees and with whom he spent his holidays whenever he could. Winifred returned with him to Sinai. That remote desert fortress, which many an intrepid explorer had looked on with some misgivings, held no terrors for Mrs Parker. She decided that she would take a piano with her to the Governor's residence, and so the two-day camel journey from Suez was accomplished with two of the beasts carrying the separated halves of the wooden-framed piano between them. Before her marriage she had travelled with Grace Kennedy Frazer collecting Scottish folk music and recording it on a phonograph. She also translated Gaelic fairy tales which were published in 1907, and collected recipes for a cookery book which was still in print in 1983.

British officers serving in the Sudan at that time were not encouraged to marry, and so he resigned his British army commission and became an officer of the Sirdar's army, with the rank of Lieut.-Colonel, which more befitted the governorship of a province however small its population – an uncounted few thousand at the time.[10] To the Arabs, among whom his reputation for even-handed justice and efficient government was already established, despite the tribes' inbred suspicion of officialdom of any description, he remained Birkil.

His sister (another Frances) was a keen suffragette, and one of his liveliest complaints was that whenever he returned home on leave he was compelled to visit her in prison to dissuade her from going on hunger strike. She became a full Colonel in the Women's Army during the First World War.

His tasks and achievements were hardly ever recorded, except in the dry official language of the annual reports of the Palestine Exploration Fund, where his administration was repeatedly praised for the safety with which archaelogists and surveyors, and Moslem and Christian pilgrims, were able to take their various paths. But a few signal comments crept into the literature of Sinai, the books and travel articles of the small band of scholar-spies and army staff officers who travelled through the wilderness in the first decade-and-a-half of the twentieth century. One of Parker's later assistants, Capt. Claude Jarvis,[11] who would succeed him as governor in years to come, wrote: 'all these outlying Arab areas were grossly maladministered with the solitary exception of Sinai, where Colonel Parker carried on with considerable difficulty, for he was starved of men, money and equipment, and it was solely due to his remarkable personality that the Government of the Peninsula was maintained.'

Jarvis also commented on the character of the self-effacing Parker who never himself told of his work even to his own family, and who in years ahead, when others wrote books and articles about their deeds in the Arab lands, quietly supported their claims rather than advance his own.

'I only ever saw Parker angry once,' wrote Jarvis. 'That was when a small police detachment was reported as being "wild and dishevelled".

' "What the hell!" shouted Parker, "You can hardly expect them to keep up the standard of the Grenadier Guards in a damned place like this." '

Birkil Bey seldom raised his voice to Arabs or fellow country-men. He was a quietly efficient soldier, a caring administrator and family man. And though he had inherited, presumably from his mother, some of the characteristics of his famous uncle, the likeness was superficial. The ice-cool Kitchener, 'a god, slightly gone to seed perhaps',[12] made no real friends in his life. His manner was distant even to his most intimate relatives and most immediate assistants, and his refusal to take part in any social

activities – other than those of Freemasonry to which he was a
devout servant – marked him off as a man apart from his fellows.
Parker was quiet but not taciturn; his gaze firm but not
chilling. And his habits had nothing of the feminine quality
ascribed to Kitchener's gestures and pursuits. Parker was a man's
man, who enjoyed the rough and tough existence of the Bedouin
as he enjoyed the sociability of the police force and the officer's
mess in Cairo. He seldom met his uncle in the 'Egyptian' years.

There were, of course, compensations in Sinai for those with
the strength and curiosity to seek them: the mountains of the
south with Jabal Musa – the 'Hill of the Law' – to attract the
followers of Juda, Muhammad and Christ, the sixth-century
monastery at its foot and the old chapel at its crown; the cloudless
magenta sky and the turquoise rocks of the north; the blue fiords
of Suez and Aqaba, and the red granite of Jabal Serbal where the
leopard still wandered in the wild.

Yet for the few Europeans who braved it, Sinai was an
inhospitable place, and they still remembered the treacherous
murder of Palmer, Gill and Charrington, and some recalled the
even earlier tribulations of the eccentric Scot, Maj. Macdonald,
who settled there with his wife in 1845, the only European in the
entire peninsula save the monks and nuns of the convents.
Macdonald spent the rest of his life at the foot of Mount Maghara
where he searched in vain for commercial quantities of turquoise,
until his death in 1870. He taught Arabs to build stone dwellings
and made rubbings of the early dynastic inscriptions which he
found as he explored and dug, and which remain to the present
day (in the British Museum) as the only testimony to a touchingly
unsuccessful life.[13]

For the youthful Governor of Sinai in the years from 1906 to
1913, however, life was spent not so much in fear of the tribes as in
an effort to understand their perverse and reckless traditions.
Among one tribe there was a custom which Parker found
comical. The exchange of words between a man and his mother-
in-law was absolutely forbidden. Generally, a wife was not
permitted to eat with her husband, and would address him not by
his name but as the father of a son or daughter. Since the

Governor was often called upon to settle family disputes, such conventions stood in the way of a western concept of law and order.

Worse, were such matters as the marriage of true-born Arabs and slaves, and the position of women claimants who, in Sinai convention, were simply lumped together with a man's meagre goods and chattels, though in a claim that she had been 'wronged', a woman's evidence was regarded as incontestable.[14]

A *cause célèbre* of 1910 involved Shaikh Sulaiman Ghonaim, who sought the opinion of Col. Parker on a delicate matter. For his pains the Shaikh was arrested and put behind bars. Sulaiman told the story as follows:

Some thirty years ago a tribesman acquired a slave. When the slave grew up he told his owner 'Times have changed, O master, I am free.' The master replied that the man could call himself king if he wished, so long as he did the work that was set for him. The slave went about his tasks, and some years later made another request. He wanted to take the hand of a girl of Sulaiman's tribe, the Awarma. The girl's father told him 'You are a Negro and can only marry a Negress.' But after the father's death the girl's brother gave her permission to marry the slave, who was now a mature if not elderly man. All my tribe felt very strongly about this, so much so that four young men set upon the slave one day as he was working underground in the turquoise mines and cut him to pieces.

Sulaiman told the story as a casual reminiscence. Parker was horrified and promptly imprisoned the Shaikh at Nakhl until he produced the murderers. 'So,' said Sulaiman, 'I eventually produced one of the young men as the murderer.' Birkil sentenced him *to five years' imprisonment*. 'Is that right? In your country, do you let the slaves marry your women?' he asked the man to whom he related the story.[15]

The youth eventually escaped from Tura prison in Cairo, and Birkil let him go. 'I consider that anyone who can escape from Tura deserves his freedom, so, when letters came through HQ asking for his recapture – I took no further steps in the matter,' said Parker. He added that the unfortunate victim of the crime was not a Negro at all, but a dark-skinned Arab who came to Sinai from Suakin.

That story was told by Col. Parker's friend G. W. Murray, the historian of Sinai and its tribes. Parker himself told other stories of the fickle people among whom he was to spend much of his adult life. 'Their love or hatred of a man they perpetuate for generations,' he said.

On the road between Nakhl and Aqaba is the grave of a person execrated by all. What his crime or failing was I have never discovered. But whenever passing the place an Arab will cast a stone on a still growing heap, spit, and utter a curse. The story goes that an old Arab lady expressed pity for the man and refused to conform to the custom, with the result that next day, while herding goats, she fell down and broke her leg.

Parker said of Musa abu Nasir, paramount shaikh of all the Arabs of southern Sinai at the time of Professor Palmer's murder that he was a man 'of great fineness and strength of character'. And he added:

The story is told of him that when Professor Palmer was murdered he was sent for by Suez (Intelligence Office). . . he was taken before a Captain of the Royal Navy, who was making the enquiry, and interrogated about the murder through an interpreter. He did not like the accusatory tone of the interpreter, and remained silent. The officer asked what was the matter. He replied that he objected to being questioned as if he had had a hand in the murder, whereas he was doing all he could to find the murderers. If he were offered a chair and a cup of coffee he would discuss matters. The chair and the coffee were provided, and the enquiry proceeded.

2
The Threads of War

Ever since the occupation of Egypt by Lord Wolseley's expeditionary force, Sinai had been seen as the buffer which stood between European ambition and the Suez Canal. Suez was the lifeline of the British Empire; the only plausible route to India and the East. Even so distant a threat as the appearance of a single German gunboat at the Moroccan port of Agadir in 1911, was looked on as an ultimate threat to Britain's position in the East.

Kitchener, denied the Viceroyalty of India which was his sole remaining ambition, turned reluctantly to Cairo. Even the King had supported his claim to Viceregal Lodge, but Morley, the Secretary of State for India, had said that the victor of Omdurman and the hero of the Boer War had become 'hopelessly idle', and refused to countenance his application. It was, perhaps, a tardy recognition of Britain's concern for the security of Suez and the protection of Egypt that an old soldier so disdained should be chosen for the task. But beneath all the outward blarney and the almost contrived appearance of ineptitude, it must be supposed that *Whitehall* knew what it was doing. That, at any rate, was what foreigners thought. British political and military intelligence was considered the most subtle, penetrating and efficient in the world in the first years of the twentieth century.

Germany, gradually restoring the glory of Prussian supremacy and sharing it out with grudging parsimony among the united states of the Hohenzollern empire, wasn't far behind. Indeed, in the Middle East (a term which came into use in 1906 when the War Office drew a line from Aqaba to Basra and awarded most of the territories south of it to Military Intelligence, Simla), Germany was very much in the ascendant. Britain and France had sweetened the pill of the 1904 *entente* by agreeing to far-reaching privileges for Germany in the Ottoman Empire and Egypt. Wilhelm II, the 'protector' of Islam who was known throughout the Arab world as 'Hajji Wilum', the Pilgrim, made sure that some of his best men were sent to the East. Indeed, the Wilhelmstrasse maintained a highly efficient Eastern Bureau which controlled political intelligence activity in all the Islamic territories, with an archaeological section which maintained contact with the distinguished academics who wandered and dug in Sinai and Palestine, Egypt, Mesopotamia and Anatolia. Germany's spies were of the highest social and scholastic calibre, as were the official ambassadors of the Reich.

The majestic von Bieberstein at the Sublime Porte, the princely Hatzfeld and Bernstorff in Egypt, approached hosts and competing ambassadors alike with winning charm and an incomparable grasp of affairs. Armed with a Prussian sense of virtue and a teutonic thoroughness they generally ran rings round their British, French and Russian counterparts. There was the highly professional, if somewhat less aristocratic, Dr Friedrich Rosen, hovering from one trouble-spot to another – Tehran, Jerusalem, Tangier – a Jewish scholar who looked at politics and a troubled world with the kindly eye of a man who preferred to contemplate poetry and philosophy and only gave his mind to human folly when he must. And there was Baron Max von Oppenheim, son of the Jewish banking family, favourite of the Kaiser and Kaiserin, dismissed in British Intelligence files as an 'egotistical' windbag. He divided his time between Egypt, Constantinople, Berlin, America and Tel Hafar (the Mesopotamian site which he began to excavate in 1906) in the decade before the outbreak of war, entertaining lavishly wherever he went and playing host with particular zest to the Pan-Islamic agents who were the spearhead of a hardening Turco-German alliance.

Such was the main opposition to imperial Britain in the east.
The Deuxième Bureau of France, notorious for its unscrupulous
and single-minded method, was represented at all the power
centres, especially Damascus, Beirut and the Persian Gulf. The
Austro-Hungarian secret service, in league with the Czar's
Okhrana through the duplicity of its chief of counter-intelligence
Col. Redl, was represented in the vast area which stretched from
Sinai to the Persian Gulf by the extraordinary Bohemian Jew
Alois Musil, a scholar traveller who knew more of inner Arabia,
its tribes and its chiefs than any other outsider. But the Kaiser's
men were the real enemy, and Britain kept a keen eye on them.

The Balkan wars of 1911–13, the tentative knitting of Entente
and Alliance, and the final victory of the Young Turks in
Constantinople, led inexorably towards a war in which Britain,
France and Russia would confront Germany, Austria–Hungary
and Turkey, with Italy and Greece hovering uncertainly between
the chief contestants; a conflagration which would be lit by the
insanely contrived spark of Sarajevo. By 1913, war was inevitable.
The only question asked by those who observed the movements of
armies and the plans of the general staff, was 'When?'

Sinai, remote from the world at large, its few thousand
tribesmen going about their daily tasks of sheep and camel
minding and the *ghazzu*, the eternal sport of the desert, the raid
of one nomad on another, provided many a clue in the uneasy last
months of peace.

There were strange comings and goings, and Parker and Alwyn
Bramly kept a weather eye on them from Cairo while the new man
at Nakhl, Capt. C. E. Barlow, maintained an official presence in
the land whose legal ownership was as uncertain as ever.[1]

July 1913 may be taken as a good month to begin to follow the
machinations of the European powers in and around the
peninsula of Sinai. It was the month in which Britain and Turkey
initialled a convention with the old-guard politicians of the
Ottoman Empire; the old liberals of the regime who had survived
the first onslaught of the brash Young Turks. It was an agreement
which served the new rulers of the empire well, however, for it
recognized Turkish hegemony in central Arabia, the vast region

of which Ibn Saud of Riyadh and Ibn Rashid of Hail had fought for the past decade.

It was the month, too, in which the Foreign Office in its effort to placate Turkey and prevent further German incursion reaffirmed its instruction to the Government of India and to British agents in the Middle East that there must be no contact with central Arabia. The Anglo-Turkish Convention had recognized Ibn Saud, the ascendant star of the desert lands, as the Ottoman mutassarif or governor of the region then known as Najd. He was not to be encouraged in the belief that he was, or could become with British support, an independent ruler.

The Government of India took a different view. While recognizing the need for a strong Ottoman buffer between Europe and the overland route to India, it also believed that Ibn Saud's tribes represented an irresistible force which would be ignored at Britain's peril. It was a belief which had been propounded for some four years past by Britain's man on the spot, Capt. William Shakespear the charismatic adventurer who occupied the political agency of Kuwait, the watchtower of the Arabian desert. He was already in secret communication with Ibn Saud, reporting with the highest confidentiality to his senior Sir Percy Cox, the Resident in the Persian Gulf, and to the Military Intelligence department at Simla. In the race to win the allegiance of the Arab leaders, a battle royal developed between the British Government in London and the Viceroy's administration in India. Peace had been signed in the Balkans. Germany had been accommodated in its plan to finance and build the Berlin–Baghdad railway. The Foreign Secretary, Sir Edward Grey, did not intend to allow men he regarded as little short of political adventurers to upset the apple cart. But Germany pressed at the door of the Gulf, in Basra and the Persian ports, and sought a base for its merchants and spies in Kuwait. The Indian Government was not willing to permit the new amity which reigned in Europe to undo the work of centuries in the East.

The internal squabble which weakened Britain's policies and its imperial will, was given a complex twist by events in the Arabian territories. In 1902, soon after his return to Riyadh, the historic centre of Saudi power in central Arabia, Abdal Aziz bin Abdurrahman, the young amir who had taken the mantle of his forefathers 'Ibn Saud', fought a battle with his namesake Abdal Aziz ibn Mitab who was known as 'Ibn Rashid'. The latter was defeated and killed, but Ibn Saud was not yet strong enough to take possession of the territory, the district of Jabal Shammar, which had been snatched from the Sauds nearly seventy years earlier. But he had given sanctuary to one of the princes of the House of Rashid, a murderous and scheming cousin of the young prince who now occupied the throne of Jabal Shammar, by the name of Faisal ibn Rashid. And Faisal ibn Rashid was in close communion with the *de facto* ruler of the Shammar tribes, whose capital, Hail, nestled amid the foothills of the Shammar mountains in the north. That ruler was the Regent Zamil ibn Subhan, who from 1909 led the tribes and administered the lands of Hail on behalf of the infant prince Saud, the son of Abdal Aziz ibn Mitab, who had been protected from his regicidal family by the Sharif of Mecca until his uncle Zamil was able to protect him.

Through the intervention of the conspiratorial Faisal, Zamil and Ibn Saud were in secret communication with the object of uniting the tribes from Sinai and Syria in the north to the Saudi homelands in the south. Thus brought together under the joint banners of Riyadh and Hail they would represent a mighty force which would ensure their independence from the Ottoman power in Constantinople. They were not rich enough, though, to stand alone, and so they sought the aid of one of the great powers. And through the bond of friendship which was forged between the Political Agent Shakespear and Ibn Saud, they turned with increasing hopefulness to Britain.

After the Young Turks' revolution of 1907, another circumstance bolstered the desire of a few religious zealots and a number of Arab officers serving in the Ottoman army for autonomy, for freedom from the oppressive hand of the Turkish mudirs and kaimakams, and from the inevitability of conscription into the Turkish army. Latching on to the lessons taught by their masters, they formed clandestine organizations which came together in the urban centres of Syria as *al Ahad*, the Covenant. Pan-Arabism –

the notion of an Arab empire – entered the minds of men whose ancestors had been governed nominally for four centuries by the Ottoman Turk and whose lives had been chiefly nomadic and thus free of all but tribal restraint. It was a notion which would excite Arabs of town and desert to courageous and wilful acts of self-assertion, and which would find in the ensuing years a singular and short-lived realization, the United Arab Republic of Quwatly's Syria and Nasser's Egypt, formally inaugurated in 1958.

If the complexities of Arab lineage are confusing to the layman, they are as nothing compared to the haphazard tapestry of Arab and imperial politics which began to take shape in the summer of 1913, and which impinged ever more insistently on Egypt and its tributary territory of Sinai. Before the month of July was out a third attempt had been made on the life of Kitchener in the two years since he took over as uncrowned 'king' of Egypt. Alongside the Pan-Arab movement there had developed a religious impulse which had a wider and more profound influence than Arab nationalism – the Pan-Islamic ideal. Indeed, the new fervour of the muftis and imams had its origins in the very beginnings of Islam and in the subsequent holy wars of the Prophet and his followers. The religious leaders and teachers of all the Islamic countries, including India and Egypt, were among its most devoted exponents. And the Young Turks, encouraged by Germany and its agents, embraced the movement as a useful stick with which to beat the infidel British.

The secret police of India and Egypt, and the military intelligence services which worked alongside them, began to find the inspiration of much of the disorder in the eastern world – which had hitherto resided in international anarchism and resurgent nationalism – in the Pan-Islamic cabals.

A thousand miles from Cairo, in the tiny principality of Muhammerah on the Persian side of the Shatt-al-Arab, a secretive meeting took place on 6–7 July 1913, aboard the monitor ship HMS *Sphinx*. The gathering was designed to brief Britain's two most reliable allies in the area, Shaikh Khazal of Muhammerah and Shaikh Mubarak of Kuwait, on the Anglo-

Turkish Convention; and to ensure their support in implementing its provisions in accordance with Britain's interpretation of them. On the British side were Percy Cox the Resident, Maj. Haworth a Simla intelligence officer seconded to Khazal as Political Agent, and Capt. Shakespear who was in disgrace after admitting to a clandestine meeting in the desert with Ibn Saud two months before. The Arab eminences were told that Germany had been given the go-ahead to build the Baghdad railway as far as the Gulf, but Britain had not shown the Turks – the owners of the territory through which the line would pass – the secret treaty it had signed with Shaikh Mubarak in 1907, which gave HM Government perpetual rights over the piece of land which provided the only suitable terminus on the north shore of Kuwait harbour.

The aged Mubarak and Khazal were no strangers to conspiratorial politics. Their lives had been devoted to devious causes. Mubarak had once been the protector of the Saudi ruling family, and he regarded the young Ibn Saud as his adoptive son. He had been instrumental in the return of the family to its capital, Riyadh. Now he was told that Ibn Saud would be left at the mercy of his bitter enemy the Turk. He went along with the scheme without protest. The Amir of Najd and all its tribes would be told that he must sign a treaty with the Turks, accepting the position of their local governor.

The Convention also recognized Ottoman control of Ibn Saud's seaboard of al Hasa, just south of Kuwait. But Ibn Saud had pre-empted the negotiators in London by leading an expeditionary force to take it from the Turks in May, soon after Shakespear's covert visit to the Saudi amir. As a parting shot, Mubarak was told that he must keep all foreigners 'at arm's length' from now on, especially Germans and Turks.

One small problem remained for Whitehall and the Sublime Porte. By meeting Turkish claims in Arabia and placating Germany in Mesopotamia, the Foreign Office hoped that it could keep Berlin and Constantinople apart, and so prevent an eastern spread of conflict should war in Europe ensue. But Ibn Saud and the Regent of Hail, Zamil, could still spoil their plans by uniting the tribes under the Pan-Arab banner and waging war against the Ottoman authority. In 1911 Shakespear had camped with Ibn Saud in the desert and reported to the Government that an Arab revolt was planned by all the desert chiefs, with Ibn Saud at its head. By 1913 that plan had been concerted with the military nationalist committee in Damascus, al Aad, and high-ranking Arab officers in the Ottoman army had become involved, the chief of them, Gen. Yasin Pasha. Another leading light was Maj. Aziz Ali al Masri, who had distinguished himself in the wars of the Balkans and North Africa. With the single exception of the Sharif of Mecca, all the conspirators accepted the leadership of Ibn Saud, but the Najdi chief's ability to command a desert revolt which had any chance of success rested on the possibility of an alliance between his tribes and those of Ibn Rashid under the control of the Regent Zamil.

They set a date in early 1915 for the raising of the banner.

Kitchener in Cairo became deeply immersed in the plots of the desert shaikhs. Arab nationalists from all sides were constant callers at the Cairo Residency, and the other European powers – notably France, Germany and Austria-Hungary – took a keen interest in the activities of the Arab protagonists.

Parker's Sinai stint came to an end in March 1912 when Wingate, the Sirdar decided to recommend to the Khedive that he should take over as Commandant of the Cairo Police School at Abbassiya and its associated spy-training establishment. If the army and intelligence men in Egypt used native titles such as *Mudir* and *Kaimakam*, consultation with the country's nominal ruler was no more than an act of courtesy. Resident and Consul-General Kitchener was in firm control of the Ministry of the Interior and all other essential instruments of government. On 24 March Wingate wrote from GHQ Egyptian Army, Khartoum:

My dear Parker:

I need not say how greatly I regret to lose your services, but, at the same time, I am confident that the new sphere into which you have now entered will prove one of usefulness to the Egyptian Government, and I hope of advantage to yourself – at any rate from the domestic point of

view, for it will enable Mrs Parker to be very much more with you than
was possible when your residence was at Nakhl. Lady Wingate joins me
in hearty congratulations and desires her kindest messages also to Mrs
Parker and yourself.

Wingate also congratulated him on the Order of Osmanieh 4th
Class 'which His Highness the Khedive has conferred upon you. . . .
I desire to very cordially thank you for all your good work in
various capacities, and especially for the way you carried out your
duties as Governor and Commandant of the Sinai Peninsula.'

In fact, the Sinai years had been spent in an almost unbroken
dispute with the military authorities in Cairo over his status.
Officially, Wallier Parker was Civil Governor of Sinai. His British
Army commission having been resigned in 1906, he remained on
the supernumerary list of the Egyptian Army, but his future
position as an officer of that force, and his pension arrangements,
were confused by the dual role he had taken on in 1906 when he
went to Sinai as civil Governor under the direct orders of the chief
of military intelligence. The matter had not been resolved by the
time of his appointment to the Police School; and it was to remain
in abeyance until the declaration of war in 1914, when he was
reinstated on the active list of the Egyptian Army. Correspondence with the Military Secretary of the Army, which began in
November 1910 through Lee Stack the DMI, stressed that though
he was perfectly happy to serve in the wilderness, he was
'sufficiently ambitious' to hope that his services would find
'greater scope and better pay' in the future. The response of the
Military Secretary in the course of the ensuing two years of
argument was a monumental example of official evasion. None
the less, he threw himself into the job with an enthusiasm that
soon earned him the soubriquet 'Sinai Parker' among his
compatriots and won him the friendship and loyalty of the tribes,
while his doughty wife Winifred turned the cold unwelcoming
fortress of Nakhl into a veritable country home. Her only
complaint was that the piano which had been lugged so laboriously
across the desert remained hopelessly out of tune.

The last rites of the planned Arab revolt were played out in the autumn of 1913 and the spring of 1914.

Britain's front door in the Middle East, Suez, was secured by the Egyptian army under its Sirdar Gen. Sir Reginald Wingate, and by the strong, taciturn regime of the Resident Kitchener, under whom Wingate had served as intelligence chief in the Sudan. It was protected too, on its eastern side, by Sudanese detachments at the fortresses of Suez, Arish, Nakhl and Aqaba, though Turkey had retained an admitted sovereignty over the peninsula in the arrangement of 1906.

Germany was kept more or less content by its domination of the Baghdad Rail consortium – from which France withdrew at the last moment under British pressure, on the understanding that it retained 'priority in Syria' – and by the granting of exclusive rights to the archaeologists of the Reich to dig in Mesopotamia. But German ambition transcended concessionary rights. Its agents set out urgently to undermine Britain in the Gulf through a commercial company known as Robert Woenckhaus; and Britain's spies in Sinai began to detect unrecognized European gentlemen on the pilgrim road to Mount Sinai. The central deserts of Arabia were left by the General Staff in Berlin and the Eastern Bureau of the German Foreign Office to their ally Franz-Josef in Vienna. His man, Alois Musil, kept up his vigil and his close contacts with the shaikhs to the bitter end. By the end of 1913, the Viceroy of India, Baron Hardinge of Penshurst, had brought intense pressure on London to permit Capt. Shakespear to make a journey across Arabia from Kuwait to Cairo, calling at Riyadh on the way. The Foreign Office had agreed to the journey, while arranging to send its own representative to the scene of action, the formidable lady traveller Gertrude Bell.[2]

By the end of that year the European powers were engaged in a frantic effort to bring the warring tribes of central Arabia to heel, and to monitor each other's activities. It was a strange scenario which evolved from the London Convention between Britain and Turkey. Both sides were anxious to kill off the threat of Arab revolt. To that end, Zamil the Regent of Hail must be deposed. Ibn Saud would thus be prevented from leading a formidable desert alliance. Whitehall decided to give approval to Gertrude Bell to make a journey to Hail, the Rashid capital, despite its recently reaffirmed ban on all travel in central Arabia. At the same time the Viceroy of India gave sanction to a journey by Capt. Shakespear diagonally across the peninsula of Arabia – a journey which would take him to Hail at almost exactly the time of Miss Bell's expected visit. The Sublime Porte, informed of these proposed journeys and in league with Britain in its attempt to prevent a tribal alliance, sent large caravans of arms to the enemy of Zamil within the House of Rashid, the chief minister Saud ibn Saleh, a preposterous youth with malformed nose and ears, squint eyes and blubber lips, who was already planning the murder of his uncle Zamil.

In March 1914 Gertrude Bell arrived at Hail where she was promptly made a house prisoner of the Rashids. The Rashid leaders were all at camp in the desert so that she was unable to meet anyone in authority except Fatimah, the Marie Antoinette of Hail, the scheming maternal grandmother of the young amir, Saud ibn Rashid. Meanwhile, Shakespear was with Ibn Saud at Riyadh. As Gertrude departed from Hail, the English Political Agent was on his way to the Rashid camp near the wells of Zarud, close to the pilgrim route, the Darb Zobaidah. Shakespear was accompanied by two agents of Ibn Saud, Saleh al Mutawah who had been Capt. Leachman's guide on his journey to Riyadh in 1912 – when that other English traveller went as the agent of the War Office to the southern power-centre of Arabia – and by Saleh's brother Ali who was Ibn Saud's chief at the township of Ayun in the contested territory of Qasim. Saleh went to the Rashid camp to warn Zamil that an attempt on his life was probable. But he was too late. On 10 April 1914, as the Regent was riding near the Rashid camp, he was shot in the back by slaves of Saud ibn Saleh. The threat of desert rebellion was over. As Shakespear went on to the Syrian desert and Sinai he observed large shipments of arms to the Minister Saud from Constantinople. He also recorded similar shipments from Austria to Ibn Shalan the paramount chief of the Anaiza tribes, who was the bitter enemy of the Rashids.

War in Europe was imminent, and the powers were jostling for position among the Arabs, lest that war should spread eastwards. Shakespear went on to Cairo where he visited Kitchener and the Sirdar Wingate on 26 May. His hosts had received another visitor a week or two earlier, Abdullah ibn Husain, the son of the Sharif of Mecca, who wanted to know if Britain would support his father's claim to the Caliphate if he rebelled against his masters in Constantinople. Shakespear found the great men of Cairo much taken up with the Sharif and quite uninterested in Ibn Saud or central Arabia. Plans for one Arab revolt had given way to the prospect of another. Turkey reinforced its garrisons at Damascus, Kerak and Maan, and other strategic points on the road to Sinai and Suez. Kitchener, who had sought the ambassadorship in Constantinople, believing that he could prevent a Turco-German alliance, left Cairo for England where he was talked into accepting the Ministry of War. His nephew left the police school he had commanded for a year to become a GSO1 (Intelligence).

3
War in Sinai

The entry of the Ottoman Empire into the First World War on the side of the Triple Alliance (which had already become a dual alliance by virtue of Italy's heel-tapping) was marked by diplomacy of the most conspiratorial kind and by strategic blunders of unthinkable magnitude.

On 2 August 1914, two days before Britain declared war on Germany and two months before Turkey finally entered the fray, a secret war alliance was forged between the Sublime Porte and the Reich in Constantinople. The pact was imposed by the will of the two strong men of the ruling Young Turks, the Committee of Union and Progress, Enver and Talaat, and Germany's aristocratic ambassador, von Wangenheim. It was resisted by the Ottoman chief minister, Prince Halim, and by the Jewish financial wizard of the Committee, Djavid. And it aroused no great enthusiasm in Berlin, where the inevitable consequence of an alliance – an insistent demand for money – was foreseen. Indeed, the Kaiser had let it be known a year before, when Enver had murdered Nazim Pasha the venerable War Minister of the Porte and usurped his office, that he would have no further dealings with the brash and ruthless men who had taken charge of the Ottoman Empire. In a sense, the Turks forced themselves on a reluctant Germany, and Britain in its maladroitness aided the alliance.

Foreign Secretary Sir Edward Grey had sent his right-hand man, Louis Mallet, to Constantinople in August to try to secure Turkish neutrality, or even Ottoman adherance to the Triple Entente. And at the insistence of the Foreign Office all British troops were withdrawn from Sinai. The fortresses of Nakhl and Aqaba were left in the charge of Bedouin police and the Sudanese troops who had preserved the peace since 1906 were sent back to their units in Egypt and the Sudan. The Turkish army was mobilized on the day of the signing of the Turco-German alliance, and the Fourth Army at Damascus, under Gen. Zakki Pasha, was instructed to make plans for an attack on the Suez Canal. Britain, in its attempt to placate the Young Turks and to ease Sir Louis Mallet's burden of negotiation at the Porte, had left the way open. The folly had been compounded by Kitchener in London, who on 9 August promised to send two infantry divisions and a cavalry brigade from India to Cairo, only to withdraw the offer nine days later after the War Office had decided to use all available Indian troops on the Western Front. At the same time, the promised reinforcement of the Maharajah of Bikanir's camel corps was also diverted to France (though the order was later rescinded), and the Egyptian commander, Maj.-Gen. the Hon. J. Byng, was told that all British troops and most of the administrative personnel in Egypt were to leave immediately for home. The troops would be replaced by territorial units. By the end of August Egypt was denuded of troops, the British commander had been replaced by Gen. Sir John Maxwell, an old hand in Egypt and the Sudan, and Germany's intelligence chief in the eastern theatre, Baron von Oppenheim, had received instructions to foster nationalist uprisings in Egypt and the Sudan. Turkish and German agents had already entered Sinai in numbers and swayed the allegiance of Bedouin police and local shaikhs with gold and extravagant promises. The Egyptian army, made up mostly of tribesmen and bereft of its British officers and administrators, stood between the Ottoman Fourth Army and the severing of Britain's 'jugular vein'.

Into September Ambassador Mallet in Constantinople insisted that the anti-war party was ascendant; that war in the East could be averted. Kitchener believed him, as did the Foreign Office. No activities in Sinai or along the Canal must be permitted which would disturb the balance of argument in Constantinople. America's ambassador, Morgenthau, knew that the matter was decided, that the Turco-German pact was a reality. So did Britain. But it was not so much the secret treaty which had decided the issue, as a naval scandal played out in the first week of war.

The *Goeben–Breslau* story has been told often enough. But the part played in the melodrama of the high seas by one man – Winston Churchill, the First Lord of the Admiralty – must be underlined, for if any individual can be said to have borne the largest share of responsibility for cementing the Turco-German alliance it was indeed Churchill. In the first fateful days of August he took the reins of operational control from the hands of his service chiefs and grasped them with all the enthusiasm of a young and inexperienced student of war games. As the two German warships – which were victualling at Messina on the day of Britain's declaration of war – made their way through the Mediterranean towards the Dardanelles, the First Lord invaded the Admiralty operations room and fired off telegrams to the C-in-C in Malta and to the commanders of HM ships giving chase. The German admiral aboard *Goeben*, Wilhelm Souchon, could not pass through the Straits of Gibraltar or through Suez. He had only one way of escape, the Dardanelles into Turkish waters. Several of Britain's faster ships of the Mediterranean fleet could have beaten the Germans to it and blocked their way. Under Churchill's instructions, they decided instead to engage in a game of hide-and-seek. The German admiral won hands down. The might of Britain's Mediterranean fleet was made to look insignificant, dwarfed by two vulnerable vessels one of which limped from gun wounds. Along the coasts of the Mediterranean crowds gathered to cheer the hunted ships, the menfolk to volunteer their services should they come into port for coal. Stripped to their waists the German stokers toiled and even gave their lives in feeding the boilers. On 10 August they sighted the plain of Troy as they passed through the Turkish straits, British warships steaming in the rear but unable to come within range. Almost all the world cheered the German victory.

Admittedly, the Chief of Naval Staff in Whitehall was by general consent a bungling amateur, the Director of Naval Operations a compliant easy-going man, and the First Sea Lord, Prince Louis of Battenburg, the victim of a vicious campaign waged by press and public against his loyalty as well as his professional ability. But in the deputy DNO, Capt. Herbert Richmond, they had the services of an officer who was acknowledged far and wide as one of the world's leading naval strategists. Richmond stood by, helpless but by no means silent, while Churchill made the operational decisions. 'We are the most appalling amateurs who ever tried to conduct a war!' he exclaimed. He was not forgiven his impudence. He was sent to Rome as Britain's naval attaché and he did not return to the scene of battle until Churchill himself was sacked from the Government.

Two months remained before Turkey finally made the move which resulted in a Russian declaration of war against the Ottoman Empire; and even then it remained for Churchill to order an act which decided the issue beyond argument and gave the enemy a precious insight into plans already being discussed in Whitehall. On 3 November, the day after the Czar's declaration of war, the C-in-C Mediterranean was ordered to make a punitive strike against the forts guarding the entrance to the Dardanelles. On 4 November, following Russia's lead, Britain and France announced a state of war.

On 16 October, Gen. Maxwell had written to Kitchener:

As we are not going to hold our Sinai frontier and will destroy as many wells as possible, I expect all the Bedouin will join the Turks if they come over. As I cannot send out patrols I do not know much about what is going on on the front lines. I expect there will be raids before long. The Turks seem to be doing a lot of work in road-making, building forts etc., all over Palestine and Syria, which looks as if they expected attack from us, but their tendency is to move south, and this can only mean attack upon Egypt. With the eight battalions from India, two mountain batteries, the Bikanir Camel Corps and the Coastguard, the Canal ought to be safe.

Still Kitchener told Cairo to be careful. No patrols must be sent into Sinai for fear of disturbing the negotiations in Constantinople.

Some 70,000 Turkish nationals in Egypt represented an immediate threat at the rear of the small British force now concentrated on the Canal. A German sailor at Alexandria swam round a British warship holding aloft the German flag and he was cheered from the shore. German officers moved into Sinai on reconnaissance missions. The Khedive of Egypt, Abbas Hilmi, was in Constantinople and on 14 November he gave his support to the *fatwa* issued three days earlier by the Shaikh-ul-Islam proclaiming *jihad*, holy war against the Allied powers. On 16 November the first contingent of Indian troops arrived at Suez and were moved up to Ismailiya and Port Said.

The Ottoman Minister of Marine, Jamal Pasha, was made Military Governor of Syria and Palestine and C-in-C of the Fourth Army. Col. Kress von Kressenstein, the young Prussian officer who retained an old-fashioned belief in gentlemanly conduct in war, took command of the crack VIII Corps which moved down from Damascus to Beersheba. A force of 20,000 men with nine batteries of field artillery and one howitzer battery was assembled.

Britain decided to send Australian and New Zealand troops, earmarked for France, to meet the challenge in Egypt. Fortuately, Gen. Maxwell had access to information from within Egypt and Sinai, from the spy network established by Parker and Jennings Bramly who had remained in Cairo and who knew more of Arab chiefs and their intentions than any one else on either side. They had already enrolled into Britain's service several shaikhs of proven reliability as well as the two most successful agents of the war in the area east of Suez, the scholarly Dominicans Father Jaussen and Father Savignac. For seven years they had wandered in Sinai, Palestine and the Hijaz, recording the ancient history and rock inscriptions of those regions, and much else. They operated from the Convent of

St Catherine on Mount Sinai, and had already mobilized many of the monks in Britain's service.

By the end of October 1914, when battle was officially joined, Kress had completed his task as Turco-German Chief of Staff. He had gathered together the reports of German agents and sent his own reconnaissance units into Sinai, and had decided to ignore the precedents of history; his invading army would march by three separate routes through the desert, avoiding the 'Way to the Philistines', the camel track through al Arish which armies had followed from the dawn of civilization, since the guns of British warships were within range. The road from Maan via Kuntilla to Nakhl – the route taken by Capt. Shakespear and carefully mapped for MO4 (the military intelligence topographical division in London) – was also under the guns of British ships anchored off Aqaba. Gen. Maxwell's agents, instructed by Parker and Jennings Bramly, had ignored London's instructions during September and October and destroyed most of the water wells of the desert. Whatever the political repercussions, the expected invading army must be denied water. But springs could be found by the Badu when the need was dire, and even by foreign invaders, as Moses discovered in the 'miracle of water'.

Col. Gilbert Clayton – 'Bertie' to his colleagues – had taken over as chief of military and civil intelligence in Cairo, on the staff of the Sirdar of the Egyptian army Gen. Wingate. Maxwell had brought with him a single staff officer, Capt. Holdich,[1] who was attached to Clayton. Parker was the senior intelligence officer under Clayton. Thus, from the outset, there was a cleavage in the intelligence service which would have bizarre consequences in the months ahead. For the moment, Clayton and his men worked in the GOC's staff HQ in the Savoy Hotel, Cairo, with a divisional office at Suez where Parker was based as GSO1. Clayton, the Director of Military Intelligence, reported to both Wingate and Maxwell, while the chief of police, Philippides Bey, ran his own secret service. The incipient division in the British camp was echoed in Jerusalem, where Jamal Pasha had installed his advance GHQ. Jamal was convinced that the Turco-German invasion would be greeted by an uprising in Egypt and he therefore set as his target the conquest of the land of the Nile. Kress von Kressenstein, a realist in a camp of hard-faced, ambitious dreamers, believed that the target should be to hold the bank of the Canal for three days at the most, to destroy Britain's lifeline and then retreat.[2]

Parker, a methodical man, kept a day-by-day diary for most of the period from 21 December 1914 until the armistice, a unique document which enables us to follow events in Sinai and later in the Arabian desert with remarkable insight. Even the names of secret agents and the fees paid to them are recorded.

The first entry shows that Maxwell had anticipated the main enemy plan, to send a small force to the south of the Sinai peninsula at Tor so as to threaten the British naval hold in the Gulf of Aqaba and the Red Sea, while concentrating its assault on the canal.

21 December 1914. Left Suez on HMS *Philomel* 3 p.m. Reached Tor 3 a.m. Searchlight. Everything apparently peaceful.

22 December. Went into harbour at daybreak. Landed and took Speakman [Capt. Speakman, quarantine officer, Tor] on board to discuss situation, nothing new. Shore again, people alarmed [at rumours of a Turkish raid] – also Monks. Nazir (Egyptian police chief) useless – no information, no posts [look-outs], no knowledge of country or Arabs. . . .

Tor, the little fishing village on the Gulf of Suez, was the quarantine township of Mount Sinai just to the north-east, and of the maritime pilgrims, and both Turkey and Britain had maintained a hygiene establishment there during their respective occupations. Its population was said to be between two and three hundred, but it changed constantly, except for a few Arab fisherfolk.

The diary for 22 December noted that the *Philomel*'s commander, Capt. Hall Thompson, had telegraphed to Suez that there was no confirmation of a Turkish raid from land or sea, and that he (Thompson) had recommended four possible courses of action: a warship to be stationed off the town; a small garrison to be set up; a Khedival (Egyptian) ship to be ready to evacuate townspeople in the event of invasion; and removal to safety of all Europeans and any Arabs or other nationals (mostly pilgrims living in the village) who wished to leave. Hall Thompson received an immediate reply. No warship available for defence or for evacuation. 'What do you recommend?' His reply recommended a party of 200 reliable men, and meanwhile he had sent ashore a small landing party.

23 December. Philomel ordered to return to Suez. The landing party embarked at 6 a.m. Ship reached Suez 3.30 p.m.

Parker was ordered to join HMS *Northbrook* (a Royal India Marine ship converted to naval service in the Red Sea flotilla) the same afternoon. Before departing on his next mission – to meet some of his Red Sea coast agents and assess the position in the Hijaz, the territory of the Sharif of Mecca and the crux of holy war – he sent his plan for Tor to Col. Bramly at GHQ Cairo. His memo reads:

1 An efficient Nazir at Tor (preferably Issairi Effendi)

2 Garrison of 200 reliable men

3 Arrangements for defence of disinfection blocks as refuge for townspeople

4 Warship to proceed to Tor on interruption of telegraph or news of attack

5 Employment of as many Arabs as possible as news agents and look-outs

6 Close liaison with Convent and issue of more rifles to the Monks

7 Employment of 'necessitous' persons at Suez.

25 December. HMS *Northbrook* left Suez at 1.30 a.m. Reached Tor about 3. *Minerva* coming up from south also came into bay. Tor peaceful. Rumour of arrival of 3 battalions of Turks at Nakhl. Intelligence informed by Speakman.

Christmas day 1914 thus came and went with only rumour of the Turco-German invasion, and no sign of the enemy. But if so much activity on the part of a senior intelligence officer centred on a fishing village in the south-west of Sinai may seem to be a trifle superfluous, Tor was in reality the key to the success of Jamal's far-reaching plan. By dominating Tor and Aqaba, the Turco-German force would be able to mine the gulfs of Suez and Aqaba, and the Red Sea.

A garrison such as Parker suggested would surely be enough to counter any enemy force capable of making the hazardous journey across desert and mountain path to Tor. But Maxwell could ill spare even 200 men from his meagre resources. By the end of 1914 another crisis – this time in the Persian Gulf, where an expeditionary force was already assembling – was sapping the strength of the Indian army. And a two-pronged German mission[3] was on its way from Berlin and Constantinople to Afghanistan, marching arrogantly across Asia Minor in one of the most daring and brilliantly planned logistic enterprises ever; a mission which would bring the imminent threat of war to the North-West Frontier. As if those events, and the threat to the Canal in Egypt were not enough, Whitehall was already planning the invasion of the Dardanelles. Maxwell's only trump card was the arrival of Australian and New Zealand troops in Egypt, earmarked for the latter campaign, whose presence was enough to muzzle thoughts of insurrection among Egyptian nationalists and the Pan-Islamites.

From 26 to 30 December, Parker's diary records *Northbrook* as 'southing' off the Hijaz coast of Arabia, where he was desperately seeking information on Turkish troop movements at the ports of Yanbo and Rabegh; and trying with as much anxiety to find and recruit suitable agents.

31 December. When off Tor sighted small boat carrying wire to be sent from Jemsa, Tor line being cut. Tor said to have been attacked. So on to Tor which reached at 1 p.m. Found that yesterday all police except Bilal and Hassan Ibrahim had deserted with rifles and ammunition after looting a shop.

He remained at the southern tip of Sinai from 31 December to 7 January organizing a temporary police force from Egyptian army men who had arrived in lieu of the British garrison he asked for, as well as sending out mountain and desert patrols. Barlow came down from Suez to discuss arrangements for defence against an unexpected Turkish attack. Telegrams back and forth along the repaired wire to Cairo show an increasing air of urgency and frustration.

3 January 1915: To Director of Intelligence, Cairo (enclosing statements of persons connected with recent happenings at Tor taken by the Egyptian *nazir*) . . . a party of six persons, previously in the employment of the Sinai Police, and some of them recent deserters, came down from Nakhl arriving in the neighbourhood of Tor on the evening of 29 December. . . On nearing Tor they went straight to the observation post under Bash-Shawish [colour sergeant] Muhammad Khawas. They there had a consultation and then cut the telegraph wire and some, if not all of them, then proceeded to Tor . . . they presently met at the house of Bash-Shawish Taka and thither by degrees collected all the police in Tor, and, by threats and inducements, persuaded them to desert. Camels were loaded with families and taken out some miles and the police followed, two of them staying behind and going to the Police Post, there waking the Nazir and giving him a letter. They then followed their comrades. Having thus got all their families clear of the town, the men returned and plundered the shop of a merchant . . . and, going back to their families, the whole party set off in the direction of Nakhl. . . . In the meantime the town was in a state of panic, the news having been put about by the deserting police that a large force of Turks was in the vicinity. All the inhabitants took refuge on the Khedival ship *Borulos* then in the harbour, embarkation going on in a rough sea from the early hours until 10 a.m. With the arrival of HMS *Northbrook* on the 31st, the inhabitants were reassured and on the morning of the 2nd [January] all disembarked and went back to their homes. As regards defection of police, it seems likely that trouble has been brewing for some time – at the same time that police at Tor deserted, the police post at Nakhl also packed up and went off . . .

A. C. Parker

4 January: Parker to Clayton, Telegram 120
Very glad to hear Barlow is coming. Already recommended by wireless
that Issairi Effendi [Arab MI agent] should replace present Nazir.
Consider it most essential for Barlow to have Issairi.

4 January: Clayton to Parker, Telegram 6108
Your 120. Afraid Issairi Effendi not available as he is on special duty on
Syrian coast. Do you think Saad Bey Rifaat would be useful if he
consents to go?

4 January: Parker to Clayton, Telegram 122
When are 200 men due?

4 January: Clayton to Parker, Telegram 6112/222
Arrangements for vessel to convey garrison to Tor are not yet quite
complete but they will probably leave Wednesday afternoon. Barlow
will go with them.

3 January: Signal HMS Minerva to HMS Northbrook, 1.30 p.m.
Arabs arrived Abu Zenima 2 Jan. directly gunboat sailed. Slight looting
private property. Interrupted by arrival Company's steamer. Six
Englishmen and ten coast guards remain, also steamer. Police departed
with looters. Shaikh Khidr states Bash-Shawish Husain of Sinai Police
arrived Jabal Tarka twelve days ago and was inducing people against
government. [Khidr, Shaikh of the Muzeina tribe, was one of the Arab
chiefs who resisted the conspiracy of 1 January.] Enclosure with *Parker
to Clayton* of 3 January. Telegraph open to Suez cut on Tor side. Hope
to repair shortly.

4 January: Parker (Tor) to Clayton (Cairo), Telegram 121
Am engaging Ghaffirs for Police town work. Cost about £30 monthly.
Have taken on 19 Arabs for observation posts at £2½ monthly. I
think we should try to get Arab shaikhs to guard roads through their
country in order to harass large parties or seize small ones. For this
purpose three commandos of 20 men each would do under selected men.
If successful each commando should receive fifty pounds monthly.
Do you approve this policy and if not please define line you wish

taken pending arrival Barlow.

4 January: Parker to Clayton: Telegram 123
Wire repaired this morning.

4 January: Parker to Capt. Westmacott, Abu Zenima: Telegram 124
What is situation? Is Shaikh Mudakhil working for you and of use? If not would like to see him here.

4 January: Parker to General Staff, Suez, Telegram 125
Shaikh Khidr should come here. Suggest he comes with Barlow.

4 January: Smith (Abu Zenima) to Parker (Tor)
Shaikh Mudakhil not working for us but will send for him to go to Tor. We arrived on 2nd, evening, and found that all houses had been broken open that day and foodstuffs, clothing, etc. looted. Many bundles left ready to move. All store houses on line to mines looted. Captain of Coastguards thinks attack will be made here by 35 of late Nakhl police . . . HMS *Minerva* called yesterday.

4 January: Parker to Clayton, Telegram 127
Smith at Abu Zenima states his officer of Coastguards expects attack by 35 men late of Sinai Police. Captain of *Northbrook* is sending *Nur al Bahr* [Egyptn lighter] if he can make wireless contact.

4 January: Parker to Capt. Smith, Abu Zenima, Telegram 126
Have wired Intelligence what you say. Police here who deserted were tricked by men who had deserted earlier. Got in touch with them in dead of night and told them that Turks were in great force in the vicinity. If you have not done so, please take statements of guardians of stores as to identity of looters.

4 January: Parker to Clayton, Telegram 129/6108
If there is any likelihood of Issairi Effendi being available later on feel convinced better wait for him . . . Also feel sure Barlow would prefer to wait for him. Fear Saad Bey Rifaat too old for task.

6 January: Capt. Smith (Abu Zenima) to Parker
Captain of Coastguards has taken statements of Ghaffirs and thinks
they acted in conjunction with Police. Eight police came and two who
were here joined them. All stores have been looted on our line of work
and expect that mines [turquoise deposits near Abu Zenima] have been
looted. Coastguards have no camels so impossible to follow and it will
mean continual trouble if Bedouins find they can rob with impunity.
Saleh Muwannas arrived last night. States you sent him for Shaikh
Khidr, is this correct? Khidr is appointed our shaikh and we would like a
responsible man in his place if he goes.

6 January: Clayton to Parker, Telegram 6116
Have sent following instructions to Barlow– 'fear impossible allow
Issairi go Tor at present but will try and find suitable officer, in
meantime must do best possible with Nazir and possibly OC Detachment
may lend officer temporarily. Relief for inhabitants. Am against issuing
grain as charity but you can spend up to £200 on relief work if necessary
pending definite arrangement. Consult with Parker and submit
suggestions to me. As regards obtaining intelligence, Parker's scheme
wants consideration. Arabs engaged for observation posts are approved
as are Ghaffirs for police work in Tor. Convent will probably help
getting intelligence through their Arabs.'

During the first days of January, while the first small emergencies
of Sinai occupied Staff HQ in Cairo and the officers on the spot,
Parker was also sending regular reports and telegrams on the
Hijaz situation to Clayton and Col. Newcombe (who had been
recalled from the Western Front to his old pitch in the Middle
East, where he had been in charge of British military intelligence
in Syria up to the declaration of war, and who now joined Parker
as GSO1 on Clayton's staff). There was little time for sleep while
the foundations were laid for the defence of Suez.

From 6 to 8 January the names of more and more Arab agents
and paid 'head men' appear in the diary. One of his men, Abdal
Momenim, is sent to Abu Zanima to set up a wireless transmitter
and receiver. From 9 to 13 January Parker is 'southing' again
aboard the *Northbrook*, looking for agents along the Red Sea

coast, before joing HMS *Himalaya* at Port Sudan for the return journey. He arrived back at Tor at 9 a.m. on 13 January.

As with trained men, ships and aeroplanes were scarce in Egypt, and the essential tasks of reconnaisance and agent-dropping were the responsibility of a brave and motley band of men under the immediate command of Newcombe and Parker. The ships, often enemy vessels commandeered at the declaration of war before they could escape port, were mostly cargo steamers converted to naval use as 'aircraft carriers' or troop and agent carriers; some were fitted with powerful radio transmitters and receivers to act as 'monitor' ships, perpetually scouring the Mediterranean and Red Sea coasts to intercept enemy signals and report on the movements of Arab tribes and the Turkish soldiers who moved among them. Their names became legendary to the men who served with them and relied on them. The outside world would never know of their exploits. His Majesty's Fleet Auxiliary *Aenne Rickmers*, for example, goes unrecorded in naval halls of fame. But the 7,000 tons *Aenne Rickmers*, a trampish German lady much loved by her captors, worked harder than almost any other vessel in the eastern theatre through thick and thin, until she was knocked out in the Dardanelles, and repaired and dignified by an anglicized name, HMS *Anne*.

The rag-tag fleet of 'spy' ships and converted carriers were all commanded by that special breed of men, RN reserve officers, mostly retired naval men who had served in the merchant marine up to the declaration of war. Perhaps the most famous of them was Lieut.-Cdr. John Kerr, the Scot with a Yankee accent who had served with the American cavalry between his two naval careers and who in a few months' time would steer the ill-fated *River Clyde* on its historic voyage to Gallipoli, laden with some of the most heroic men of that most feckless campaign. Kerr would later command the *Aenne Rickmers* when she became the *Anne*. But not even that intrepid sea-warrior could excel the colourful exploits of *Aenne Rickmers'* first captain, the 6ft. 2in., 23-stone Englishman Lieut. 'Dick' Gaskell, and his Greek crew, French pilots and mechanics, English chief engineer and observers, and Irish intelligence officer who was the operational CO.

Men who served on such ships were given an extra allowance to compensate for the discomforts and dangers of their work. It was called 'hard lying'. Only the finest seamen and most able intelligence officers could take part in the secret missions of the 'spy' ships, for they operated along unlit coasts and in largely uncharted waters; and discovery in their work of dropping agents behind enemy lines had only two penalties, hanging or the firing-line.

Capt. L. B. Weldon joined the *Aenne Rickmers* in the first days of January 1915. He had been doing map work in the intelligence office at the Savoy Hotel in Cairo since August of the previous year. When 'Skinface' Newcombe arrived, along with two young staff lieutenants named Lawrence and Woolley, on Christmas eve of that year, he (Newcombe) took Weldon under his wing and sent him down to Ismailiya where he would receive instructions from Col. Jennings Bramly. He was told that he would be joining the *Aenne Rickmers* as its military CO.[4] He would be responsible for planting agents along the Syrian and Red Sea coasts, reporting to Newcombe in the former case, and to Parker in connection with Sinai and Hijaz missions. He would also be responsible for seaplane missions undertaken by the French pilots Grall and de l'Escaille with their English observers Capt. J. R. Herbert and Capt. T. J. Todd.[5]

The first task of the Irishman Weldon was to establish a rapport with his multinational army and navy crew. A strong, fit man, his hand was almost crushed by the vigorous grasp of the ship's captain. On the wall of the captain's cabin he noticed a photograph of a most attractive young woman whom he assumed to be Gaskell's wife. It turned out to be Aenne Rickmers, the beautiful daughter of the ship's legitimate owner, Herr Rickmers of Hamburg. Five Bluejackets and six marines were aboard to provide assistance ashore, or in the event of going aground and being attacked. The seaplanes carried by the old German steamer had begun reconnoitring into the Sinai and Moab deserts before Weldon joined her. The frail planes – Henri Farmans fitted with floats filled with inflated bladders – were transported by *Aenne Rickmers* into the Gulf of Aqaba, from where they took off for

Wadi Araba in the direction of the Hijaz railroad. But the high mountain range which separates southern Syria as it was then (Transjordan or Jordan of the present day) from Arabia proper, was a dangerous obstacle. De l'Escaille, Grall and the other pilots were determined to surmount the hills, however, in order to observe the Turkish garrison at the main base of Maan.

In early January, a plane piloted by Lieut. Grall with Capt. Stirling, late of the Dublin Fuseliers, as his observer, overstretched its 80-hp engine and was forced down in Wadi Araba on the return journey, 29 miles from the sea. Weldon sent a party of Bluejackets to the rescue and they found the French pilot dead; his English companion was injured and almost fried to a turn by the terrible heat of the desert, but he was brought to safety. Sir John Maxwell promptly issued an order forbidding any further attempts at surmounting the mountains of Moab. However, reconnaisance of Sinai and the coastal strip of Arabia continued between the other and even more dangerous enterprises of the 'Annie'.

Other sorties into Turkish-held territory were carried out by land-based craft, again mostly Farmans but with the reinforcement of a single B.E2a from India. The only aerodrome was at Ismailiya on the canal, with a landing-ground at Kantara some 20 miles to the north. When long flights into Sinai were intended, troops were sent out in advance to prepare landing-strips several miles into the desert, in case the precious planes and their even more precious pilots were unable to reach the canal. Pilots and observers knew that if they fell short of the strips, or their permanent base, they were doomed to certain death from sun or tribes.

The ever-present danger of torture and death which threatened the officer and agents of military intelligence in the desert war seemed to attract men of fiery and sometimes perverse conviction; men who would sacrifice life and limb in the service of King and Empire, yet in some notable cases devote the rest of their lives to republicanism and the destruction of everything empire stood for. Among the men employed by Parker and Newcombe at this time on the little ships and seaplanes which dropped spies, leaflets, bombs and other objects in Syria, Sinai and the Hijaz, were Captains Erskine Childers and William Wedgwood Benn. Both men were aboard HMFA *Ben-my-chree* which made innumerable visits to the Crusader citadel of Athlit on the Palestinian coast where a small but highly effective Jewish spy-ring operated under the direction of the most brilliant of all Britain's wartime agents in the area, Aaron Aaronsohn. On one mission it carried ten aircraft which all took to the air at the same time, destroying the Turkish rail junction of al Afuleh.

The worthy *Ben-my-chree* was eventually sunk by an enemy torpedo. Wedgwood Benn was awarded the DSO for gallantry in the engagement, and went home to set a family tradition of off-beat radicalism. Erskine Childers, the intelligence officer aboard the ship, became a Sinn Feiner. The Squadron Commander of the seaplane carriers was C. l'Estrange Malone who became an active Communist. Eccentricity was not confined to the serving officers of that courageous band which played such havoc with enemy and friends in the desert war. By an arrangement which only the British could contrive in the most desperate moments of war the 'spy' ships were the property not of the Royal Navy but of the Ports and Lights Administration in Cairo, though they came under the control of the GOC. The appellation 'HM' came only after their transfer to the navy in August 1915.

After the invasion of Egypt by the Turco-German army of Jamal Pasha had been repulsed, Capt. Weldon was asked to give a Christmas-time talk to the men aboard *Ben-my-chree*. He was asked to describe the Sinai desert. 'Only three men ever really knew Sinai,' he replied, 'Moses, Napoleon and Col. Parker.'

For the moment, in January 1915, Parker was still at the southern tip of Sinai, dealing with the Arab insurgents at Tor and Abu Zenima. He would shortly be called on to demonstrate his familiarity with its perverse inhabitants and its unmapped byways.

On 19 January while in Cairo, Parker discussed the likely routes of a Turco-German invasion with Stewart Newcombe. The lean sapper who had recently arrived in Cairo was familiar with the eastern edge of Sinai which he had surveyed with the young archaeologists Leonard Woolley and Thomas Lawrence early in 1914. Those two assistants, who had been called down from the Hittite site at Carchemish to take part in their first espionage venture, were now working for Newcombe. Woolley was sent up to the Port Said intelligence office while Lawrence did map work in the Savoy Hotel. After his discussion with Newcombe, Parker put his thoughts in writing, suggesting that the probable enemy advance would come along the Katia road from Arish and that Jamal would then face two choices, a bald-headed attack on the Canal or a nibbling attack in the hope of a nationalist rising within Egypt. He was wrong on the first count. The German staff officers had anticipated such an assumption. But he was right in his belief that the Turkish commander, a political general if ever there was one, might place his faith in a pro-Turk rebellion. The crushing of that hope condemned the campaign to failure before it began.

The attack on the Canal zone was substantial in its planning and organization and desultory at the last. In the final week of January 1915 Jamal's army of 20,000 men moved off from Beersheba with the assistance of a moon which approached fulness, 'disregarding all the precedents', as its Chief of Staff was to declare in later years. Some 5,000 camels carried water for the invaders who marched by the cool of night, when aircraft could not reconnoitre, through Wadi Arish, Al Auja and Libni, and between the hills of Maghara and Yelleg towards Ismailiya. Smaller diversionary forces moved along more conventional routes by Al Arish on the coast towards Kantara, and by Nakhl in the direction of Suez; but they did not mislead the British force that waited for them. As the main army dragged its field artillery and howitzers across the central plain of Sinai, with its vast camel-train bringing supplies of food, water and ammunition, it was spotted first by Parker's agents and then pin-pointed at its daytime halts by the planes from Ismailiya. Bombs caused panic among the Turco-German army (which consisted mostly of Arabs). But the staff work of Kress and his men was good. They had plotted their route well, and had established a useful network of spies. Generally they camped in the protective shadow of hill or wadi, or spread themselves thinly. Despite almost continuous daytime bombing attacks, Jamal's army lost not a single man or beast on its crossing of Sinai, though the small 20-pound bombs of the British and French aircraft dropped all around and sent puffs of sand into the air which effectively concealed the enemy from follow-up attacks.

Jamal had staked everything on a surprise attack, hoping that he could hold a stretch of the canal on its east bank south of Ismailiya with five or six thousand men 'at the first rush'. He would then bring up the 10th Division, giving him a force of ten thousand rifles with which to dig in on the far bank. Ismailiya would be taken and occupied for four or five days, while the 8th Division, held back at Beersheba, was rushed across the desert.

But the element of surprise was lost by Jamal before the battle was joined and the British force, consisting chiefly of Indian army troops, waited confidently.

On 1 February sightings of the enemy were made at Bir Habeita (some 2,500 infantry with two guns), Moyat Harab (8,000 men), Bir al Mahadat near Al Ferdan (3,000 men). In the palm grove of Bir al Dueidar near Kantara a few hundred infantry seemed to be hiding, but many more could have been concealed by the trees. Other forces, considerable in numbers, had assembled at Arish and Nakhl. On the 2nd, early morning patrols reported that the main enemy force had sent an advance detachment forward towards the Ismailiya ferry-post during the night. Contact between the opposing forces was made at 3.30 p.m. on that day. British ships in the Mediterranean, in the Canal itself, and in the Gulfs of Aqaba and Suez, shelled the Turks with devastating power whenever they came within range.

The events of that first day of tentative desert warfare were summed up by a French officer on duty at the ferry-post of Ismailiya.

On the hills, ten or fifteen kilometres from the Canal, we could see numerous traces on the sand of the columns that had moved forward during the night. But in the plain there was nothing. The desert, in its high light, looked like a smooth cloth, but was in reality cut by numerous depressions in which troops could be hidden. The first patrols which moved out were met by rifle fire. They were reinforced; then artillery was sent out to their support. At my side was a battery of Indian mountain artillery, commanded by a young English officer, the only European in it. He had just been ordered to go forward. A sharp command and, in a few seconds, before we could see how it was done, the guns which had been in position were packed on the mules and the column was on the move. Meanwhile, there had sprung up a sandstorm which hid everything from view. I went out on to a dune with the English Colonel in command of the post. But there it was even worse. Even to keep one's eyes open was a horrible torture. And to think that people were fighting out in that. In the evening the detachments came in, one after another, the officers cursing the sand, the wind and the enemy, who had fallen back before them. Then quiet fell and we began to think there had been a false alarm.[6]

The alarm was not false. The sandstorm blew fiercely into the night and at 3.25 on the morning of 3 February Indian patrols, their faces screened in their puggarees, their rifles wrapped in rags to protect them from sand, peered into the darkness from the observation post at Tussum, where the main attack was expected, and heard an enemy column moving quietly towards the Canal bank. They were given away by Arab irregulars in the Turkish force who ignored the command of silence and shouted the slogan of holy war as they approached their objective: *Allah Akbar*! God is Great!

They were raked with machine-gun fire for their piety and indiscretion.

Gradually the dust storm subsided and the moon, two days from full, illuminated the Canal and the desert and silhouetted working-parties were seen to be moving towards the water, hauling heavy objects as they went. They were pontoon squads and soon the Canal was thick with them. But the 5th battery of Egyptian artillery had dug in the day before on high ground on the west bank and the first two pontoons to make their way towards the west bank were put out of action. Of twenty-five pontoons counted after the moonlight battle, only three reached the far bank.

The British force defending the Canal between the Great Bitter Lake in the south and Lake Timsah in the north consisted of: the 19th Lancashire Battery RFA with four 15-pounders; 5th Battery Egyptian Artillery with four mountain guns and two maxims; 1st Field Company East Lancashire REs (two sections); 22nd Indian Infantry Brigade consisting of 62nd and 92nd Punjabis, 2/10th Gurkha Rifles; 2nd QVO Rajputs; two platoons of the 128th Pioneers (attached to the Egyptian battery); and the 137th Indian Field Ambulance. Six companies were on the east bank, while the west bank was protected by eleven posts each held by two platoons, with sentry posts every 200 yards. Two gallant attacking forces managed to cross the Canal in the hours before daybreak. They reached the west bank just south of Tussum Post. The first was charged with bayonet by the Punjabis under Maj. Skeen, and all were killed or injured. The second was intercepted by Punjabis and Pioneers under Capt. Morgan and Lieut. FitzGibbon from Post 5. The latter officer was mortally wounded but he ran back to the post with a message for the Egyptian battery before succumbing to his wounds. Six Turks were killed and four injured. Twenty escaped and hid under the Canal bank where they were captured by the Rajputs. The two small parties which crossed the Suez Canal that night were the only enemy troops to do so in the course of the war, except as prisoners-of-war.

Iron pontoons, each capable of holding about twenty men, lay derelict alongside their dead occupants on the east bank. Jamal's surprise crossing of the Canal had been a total failure.

Battle raged through the third day of February. Merchant ships at anchor in Lake Timsah stood as silent sentinels while to the south Turkish infantry, emerging in waves from the undulating desert, launched an attack on Tussum Post and the warships *Hardinge* and *Requin* shelled them from the Canal. The Turks had secured an entrenched position only 200 yards south of Tussum Post, while 350 of their comrades had occupied British day trenches south of the post. Not until 3.30 p.m. had the Punjabis regained the positions. Gradually a British force moved up from Deversoir at the head of the Bitter Lake to Serapeum. Gurkhas,

Rajputs and Punjabis collected together to remove the Turks still around Tussum. As they advanced the enemy appeared in unexpected numbers from behind sandhills and a large Turkish force suddenly appeared in the open some three miles north-east of Tussum and began to move towards the now weakened garrison at Serapeum Post. A small force of the 2/10th Gurkhas neverthe-less held its ground against a vastly superior enemy, and with the aid of covering fire from the French warships *Requin* and *D'Entrecasteaux,* the Turks were forced to retreat. *Hardinge,* the Royal India Mail ship now armed and designated HMS, was shelled by German howitzers and its aerial mast and forward funnel carried away.

The small Turkish forces which advanced on Ismailiya to the north of the main engagement and on Suez to the south were no more than nuisance raiders. By the evening of the 3rd firing had ceased. Next day the Turks were seen to be in retreat though there were pockets of resistance and a few acts of aggression. In the following week Jamal's army went back the way it had come, and Turkey's German allies never ceased to make fun at the expense of its sanguine commander. In Egypt the effect of the news of the first famous victory of the war was described as 'excellent'. British and Indian casualties were 32 dead and 130 injured. According to German sources, 192 Turkish soldiers were killed, 371 wounded and 727 missing. British estimates put the enemy's losses, including several hundred Bedouin pressed into service, at about 2,000.

It was not quite the end of the affair, however. The diary for January showed Parker off the northern Hijaz coast from the 9th to the 12th of the month.

13th January. Reached Tor 9 a.m. Left at 5 p.m.

14th January. Reached Abu Zenima 6.30 a.m. Left 9.15 for Suez. Reached Suez 2 p.m. and Cairo 11.30 p.m.

He was at staff HQ, Cairo until 26 January when he left on the night train for Suez. Before the Canal battle raged to the north he was engaged in the appointment of agents to accompany Capt. Stirling to Aqaba on the seaplane mission which resulted in that officer's forced landing in the desert while attempting to fly over the Turkish garrison at Maan. His accounts book records:

1 February. To three men for work at Aqaba with Captain Stirling £1.500. [Payment in those days was made in both sterling and Turkish pounds.]

6 February. Left Suez in HMY *Managam.*

Managam was another of the little 'spy' ships, which carried out monitoring and agent-dropping work in the Red Sea and Mediterranean throughout the war under the command, at this time, of Lt.-Cmdr. Morewood RNR.

Relations between Parker and his chief, Clayton, seem to have been strained during the twelve days which he spent in Cairo. Clayton was preoccupied with the expected assault on the Canal; Parker was worried about southern Sinai where there were signs of Turkish infiltration among both the tribes and the small garrison of Egyptian troops left at Tor. On 23 January Parker wrote:

My dear Clayton,

I am much worried about Tor and cannot help thinking we are running a very serious risk of disaster there. As I read the wire from Barlow we have apparently lost all touch with the Arabs . . . Also there seems to be a divergence of opinion, and Barlow, who should be in a position from his local knowledge of being able to judge things at their face value, is obviously dissatisfied, though it is not clear with what. The fact of our people not adventuring to attack 150 men with at least 350 at their disposal appears to mean that there is a disinclination to entirely trust our Egyptian troops there. . . . If this is the case our inactivity against the enemy . . . is likely to foster disaffection. . . . It is difficult to see how the presence of a ship in the harbour [the light cruiser *Minerva* was at anchor off Tor] and a garrison sitting tight behind its defences is to prevent the looting of the town at night, unless we are prepared to destroy our own people's buildings with shell fire. I will not apologise for importuning you on this subject since you will understand I cannot rest quiet without explaining risks which seem very real to me.

Yours sincerely,

A. C. P.

Reconnaissance planes and agents had reported that a Turkish-led force of unknown numbers had made its way to the south of Sinai and was camped in the vicinity of Tor. Barlow, in charge of the Egyptian garrison, could not, it seemed, trust his troops to attack them. HMS *Minerva* was recalled to Suez. Parker arrived at Tor on 7 February and remained ashore for an hour, where he discovered that Barlow had no definite information on the size or whereabouts of the enemy force. It was known, however, that there were two German-speaking officers with the Turks and Arabs, one of whom was, in fact, an Austrian who had worked in the mines. Parker went up to Abu Zenima in the early morning of 8 February and was fired on by a sniper as he went ashore. He rejoined the *Managam* as 8.10 a.m. and returned to Suez. He wired Clayton from the *Managam*.

8.2.15 Telegram to Director of Intelligence, Cairo

The situation at Tor is most unsatisfactory. Nothing new is known about the enemy, but the numbers are estimated at from 80 to 150 including Arabs and they are supposed to be at the spot where they were first located by reconnaissance. They are said to have sent for reinforcements and guns. One of the two German officers is said to be away at present.

Every effort is being made to inspire garrison and people of Tor with disloyalty, and several letters have been found evidently with this object in view, the last addressed by name to the OC No. 2 Company. . . . It is said that after the first reconnaissance the enemy had orders not to fire on Egyptian troops. The fact that there has been no heavy firing on the garrison at night leads me to suppose that the enemy hopes to succeed by intrigue. The [Egyptian] garrison is strongly placed, but is hampered by buildings to the front and on the right flank. . . . The water supply could be cut without much difficulty at night. . . . The presence of monks who desire to communicate with the Convent and of townspeople who often wish to go to their houses in the town, makes it extremely difficult to ensure that no undesirable outside influence is introduced. Nearly all the houses in the town have been broken into and ransacked, as well as the pharmacy and hospital in the Quarantine enclosure.

Finally Parker made his own recommendations for dealing with a situation which seemed to be evolving from a pin-prick to a minor crisis in the Sinai campaign.

In my opinion the present situation contains very dangerous elements, which can be obviated in two ways; the entire abandonment of Tor and the withdrawal of the garrison; the sending of a sufficiently strong party of Gurkhas or British to ensure the destruction of the enemy. The first would entail an incalculable loss of prestige among Egyptians and Muhammadans who know Tor as a pilgrim station,[7] as well as among Russians who regard the Convent and its environs as a holy place.

It was the international importance of the Mount of Moses and the Convent at its foot which finally decided the General Staff in Cairo to take action. Parker had discovered from his informants – monks working for Father Jaussen – that the Turkish camp was at the rear of Jabal Hammam, among the hills of Saidna Musa (our Lord Moses), in the Wadi of Al Sidd.

'Unless reinforcements reach enemy, a double company of Gurkhas should be sufficient,' Parker had told Clayton. He added, 'the arrival of the ship or the disembarkation of men should be by night to avoid the possibility of alarming the enemy'.

11 February, Suez. Proceeded in HMS *Minerva* 12 noon. Two double companies Gurkhas, Col. Haldane, Capt. Wilson, Capt. Exham, Maj. Dickinson. Reached Tor 10.30 p.m.

12 February. Disembarked all men by 12.30 a.m. Marched to north of Al Awai and attacked and destroyed enemy at Al Sidd. 60 killed. 100 prisoners. 1 Gurkha killed, 1 wounded. Returned to Tor 1.30 p.m.

It was a matter-of-fact statement.

It was Parker and Zaidan, the son of the pro-British Shaikh Mudakhil, who led Haldane's Gurkhas to the enemy camp in the still of night. There was no moon. Only an occasional cluster of stars penetrated the cloudy sky. The Gurkhas took up position around the camp and just before daybreak the Arab sentries were overwhelmed.

The camp was rushed at dawn. A few Arabs escaped with the shaikh of the Awarma tribe, Suleiman Ghonaim who threw in his lot with the Turks at the insurrection of 1 January. They were accompanied by the Austrian, who was known as Gondos, and made their way up the coast to Abu Zenima. Of the rest, most died in their beds. Few shots were fired, for the Gurkha prefers to use his *kukri*. Many lay where they slept, their disembowled bodies paying ghastly testimony to the proficiency of a regimental force which is perhaps the most feared in the world, and to the folly of further resistance. One Arab present at that early morning carnage took the lesson to heart. The Gurkhas were dispatching the severely wounded as is their custom. The Arab grabbed the entrails of a dead comrade and laid them over his own naked stomach with such effect that the little soldiers of Nepal were deceived. They left him for dead and as soon as they departed he ran as he had never run before across the Qa'a plain to the safety of his tribe.

Old Shaikh Mudakhil had watched the proceedings from the deck of the *Minerva,* though he was not able to see the brief battle which was too far away. Several years before he had entered into a contract with another shaikh, Ayid, who contested the leadership of his tribe. Each murdered the other's father, so that they would fight alone for the allegiance of their fellows. Ayid had gone over to the Turks and was killed by the Gurkhas. Mudakhil, as he stood on the upper deck of *Minerva* as Parker's guest, at last inherited the undisputed leadership of his tribe. Nearly all the Arabs who had gone over to the Turks died, including Husain of the Awarma tribe, the Shaikh ad-Deir (tribal representative in dealings with the Convent), who had been misled by promises of gold and preferment.

There was a witness to the battle scene soon after the Gurkhas had done their work. The *Hardinge*, still scarred from the Turkish shells which penetrated the forward engine room and hit one of its funnels, visited Tor towards the end of March. Capt. T. M. Salter RN, then the ship's paymaster, went ashore with a naval party, and on the 27th he wrote to his parents:

We went down to Tor on Wednesday and yesterday I went with two other fellows to see the Turkish camp where they were caught by the Gurkhas the other day. It was a six mile tramp over the desert, but the CO troops got some camels and sent them out to meet us, and we came back en caravan. The local camel saddles are very uncomfortable and I feel very stiff and sore today. The expedition against them was remarkably well organised. The Ghurkhas were landed at Tor from a man-of-war at about midnight, no lights were shown, and they managed, after a twelve mile march, to get round the other side of the Turks' camp and surprise them at daybreak. The Gypsy troops were placed to cut them off if they made for the plain. The camp itself was in a horse-shoe shaped gully, with the mouth open to the plain, and with a steep exit up a sort of dry waterfall at the other end. The two German officers who had been with them had gone back to Nakhl a few days earlier, or probably they would have been keeping a better look out. As it was, the Ghurkas got right on top of them and the camp shows that there was some gruesome work with kukris. About 100 prisoners were taken and 70 killed while only five managed to escape into the hills. Everything in the camp which wasn't of use had been burnt so there wasn't much to see. They had an elaborate mud oven and we found the charred remains of all sorts of odds and ends, a clock, lamps, umbrellas! and a Kodak film spool. There were a lot of German cardboard cartridge boxes lying around, and fired cartridges belonging to both sides. There was one of our 4.7 shells, which hadn't burst, it had evidently been carried up to the camp, as I am afraid our bombardment (naval) had been very wide of the mark.[8]

Capt. Salter's account does not agree in every detail with the official version but it gives some idea of the bold, stealthy night march across the desert which Parker led and which took the

Turks so much by surprise that they were wiped out almost to a man.

The *Minerva* returned to Suez with Col. Haldane and the Gurkhas, and the CO paid handsome tribute to the part played by Col. Parker in the affray at Tor.[9] But Parker was not aboard. He went up to Abu Zanima aboard the *Managam*. The Turks and Arabs and their German-speaking companions had taken over the town and heavy gunfire prevented Parker from going ashore. Hamid Hamaid, a fourteen-year-old boy, gave an eye-witness account of the temporary occupation:[10]

I was asleep with the watchmen at Abu Zenima, when Suleiman Ghoneim came with the German [Gondos] and nineteen Turks on foot and six Arabs on camels. Suleiman boxed my ears, which woke me up, and then told me to carry his gun. He said to the watchman, 'O Aleiqat, your fathers are here!' and added, 'If Abu Dagn [Westmacott who had been manager of the Sinai shipping office before joining the army] were here, I would cut off his head with this sword!' Early in the morning, Suleiman and a soldier got up and lit a fire in a locomotive [a single-track line ran from Abu Zenima to the mines at Um Bogma]. Then he brought two trucks and fastened them to a locomotive, and filled them with blankets and other loot. Then the Government steamer *Managam* came in sight, and they abandoned everything and fled up Wadi Matalla. I took some dates and native butter, and fled up Wadi Tayiba. Then they fired at the *Managam* without effect and it went away northwards. When it had passed, they came back and I came back too. Many Arabs joined them when they heard that looting was going on. Then they opened the store room, and found nothing important except four boxes of gelignite which they threw into the sea. They tried to get the locomotive to start, but they couldn't. They broke up all the locomotives as far as possible with hammers and set fire to the houses. They poured oil on the [stationary] engines and set fire to them too, they took everything away on camels and stayed four days at the railhead. Then they stayed two days on the mouth of the Wadi Baba, and bought three sheep. Then news came of the fight at Tor, when they left the sheep and fled. Suleiman and the Awarma went over the Naqib Budra to their own country in Wadi Sidri. The Turks and Gondos went up Wadi

Nakhl and over Naqib al-Reikna to Nakhl. Tafeih and Amadi [two local thieves] stole the three sheep.

That youthful recollection was the last known account by an observer of the battle in southern Sinai.

The Turks were not pursued through the peninsula, for by March 1915 the Dardanelles adventure had begun and all available troops were needed to feed the voracious appetite of its commanders. Pockets of resistance remained at Aqaba, Nakhl and Arish, and sorties continued to be made against the Canal and its defences.

Parker's Sinai diary concludes:

13 February. Reached Abu Zenima at daybreak. All plant burnt. Reached Suez 3 p.m.

19 February. Left Suez in HMS *Minerva* 10 p.m.

20 February. Reached Abu Zenima 6.30 a.m. Loco put into working order and reconnaissance made to railhead by Maj. Morton, Smith, Mackenna and self, with Barnford and Westmacott running the engine, guard of six rifles. Returned about 5.30 p.m.

21 February. Left Abu Zenima 8.10 a.m, reached railhead 10.30. Bogma 5 p.m. (the manganese mining area) and camp in Um Sobesha at 6. Last parties in at half past seven.

22 February. Marched down W. Shillal leaving camp at 7.10. Reached W. Baba at 10 a.m. Left 10.25 . . . reached railhead at ll.15. Party coming over hill arriving at same time. Left by rail about noon. Going up incline Arab boy caught and dragged under wheel and terribly crushed; died almost immediately. Abu Zenima about 1.30 p.m.

23 February. Reached Suez early morning.

13 March. Inspection of 30th Brigade by Maxwell and others.

22 March. Canal attacked north of Kubri by 400 men.

23 March. Attacked enemy in Wadi Al Haj. 16 casualties.

4
General Staff, Cairo

Arab nationalism grew on the soil of revolution within the Turkish Empire, subjects following the lead of their new masters, the Young Turks.

The rebellion planned by Arab officers of the Ottoman army and their civilian compatriots through the 'Committees' of Damascus, Baghdad and Basra met a stumbling block early in 1914. The death of Zamil, which changed with a single gunshot the balance of power in the desert, and which brought a procession of European observers to the scene as if with foreknowledge of the event, prevented the planned alliance of the great tribes loyal to the Sauds of Riyadh and the Rashids of Hail. Ibn Saud was driven by Turkey and Britain into recognizing Ottoman sovereignty over his lands. Ibn Rashid swore loyalty to the Turk, and enmity towards Ibn Saud.[1] But in October 1914, as Britain's efforts to neutralize Turkey failed and the Ottoman Empire made an expedient compact with Germany, Whitehall decided that Ibn Saud might yet make a useful ally if he could nullify the army of Ibn Rashid. The Turks, for their part, were anxious to strike an early blow at Ibn Saud who made clear his sympathy towards Britain. And so, Capt. Shakespear was sent back to Arabia as Political Officer on Special Duty, and the armies of Riyadh and Hail closed on the battlefield of Tarafiya.

It was on 24 January 1915, as the British army on the Canal

waited for Jamal's troops to appear in Sinai and the British in Mesopotamia made their first tentative advances in the other campaign of the Arab lands, that battle was joined at an unmapped place called Jarab on the plain of Tarafiya. Some of Ibn Saud's troops deserted at the height of the cavalry encounter. Shakespear was left alone on a hill-top where, by a final irony of desert politics, he was shot and cut down by the very slave who had killed the Regent Zamil when Shakespear waited at Zarud almost exactly a year before. The flirtation with the prince of Riyadh was at an end. Britain turned to a new ally in the Arabian peninsula: Husain ibn Ali, the Sharif of Mecca, whom the Young Turks had nominated to his important post as the guardian of the holiest cities of Islam, at the moment of their victory in 1907.

By the time Col. Parker arrived at Staff HQ in Cairo in late February 1915, new faces had appeared at the Savoy Hotel, and whispered conversations in clubs and bars were much concerned with 'The Shareef'.

Cairo at that time was a bewildering place. The Gallipoli adventure which caused ructions in the highest councils of Whitehall, had brought thousands of Australians and New Zealanders to join the British and Indian troops who thronged the streets and bazaars, and made every day a festival for the belly-dancers and bar and brothel owners. Wide-brimmed hats, open-tunics and unfamiliar accents vied with spit-and-polish and the ejaculatory parade-ground chants of the grammar-school officers. A British intelligence officer likened Staff HQ at the Savoy to an oriental railway station. But none of the known categories of a large wartime army could accommodate another and very special brand of officer who came on stage at the beginning of 1915.

At the end of 1914, as already noted, Col. Newcombe, Parker's pre-war colleague in Egypt, was recalled to his old haunts from France where he had already won the DSO. He brought with him the two men who had worked for him in Syria as civilians, Lawrence and Woolley, scholars of Oxford University who had from the earliest days of their apprenticeship in archaeology worked under the paternal guidance of Dr David Hogarth the keeper of the Ashmolean. They were joined by another of the pre-war civilian agents in the Arab lands, Aubrey Herbert, who suffered from an eye disease which worsened year by year until he was practically blind. Already waiting in Cairo to join their number was the ex-correspondent of *The Times* in Constantinople, Philip Graves. And in their wake came the one woman in a clever, eccentric and opinionated fraternity, Gertrude Bell; and a little later still, the dapper diplomat who had received his early training in Constantinople, George Lloyd. They lived in the staff dormitory, the Grand Continental Hotel, and worked next door at the Savoy, mostly wearing the twin pips of the lieutenant and never fearing to address senior officers of the regular army with condescension or scorn.

They clustered round the Oriental Secretary of Kitchener's administration in Cairo, Sir Ronald Storrs, whose urbane, fastidious and outrageously snobbish charm fixed them all in its embrace; became their intellectual anchorage and led them into a political adventure which was begun by the old chief himself.

Eventually, Hogarth arrived in Cairo to take charge of the erudite newcomers at the Savoy Hotel who spent most of their time in archaeological and classical debate. He wore the uniform of a Lieut. Cmdr RNVR, and acted not for the military staff but for the chief of naval intelligence in London, the redoubtable, Capt. Reginald 'Blinker' Hall. Hogarth, Gertrude Bell, Lawrence and Storrs, were the most articulate operatives of an intelligence service who ever gathered in time of war, and they were to chronicle – often with subjective bias but always colourfully – the events which ensued from the débâcle of the Dardanelles and from Britain's decision to encourage the Sharif of Mecca to declare an Arab rebellion.

Parker was to record in his diary the gritty facts of the war in Sinai, Syria and Arabia. Others would add the grace notes. The threat to the Suez Canal had been swept aside. But it had not disappeared. On 21 February 1915 one of the French seaplanes was sent on another dangerous reconnaissance to Beersheba and reported that there were some 30,000 troops still gathered there. On the 23rd a reconnaissance reported 250 tents at Nakhl and other signs of military occupation at Bir Hassana between Nakhl and Arish. Maxwell, the GOC, cabled Kitchener in London: 'It would appear that we may look for another attack later on.'[2]

Deep reconnaissance by the precious planes of the Anglo-French force had already proved costly. Parker's immediate task from February 1915 was to find reliable Arab agents, some to work under his personal direction, others to operate within Father Jaussen's network which embraced many of the monks of St Catherine's, as well as Arabs all along the Red Sea coast. Parker spent the spring and summer of 1915 in securing Sinai from surprise attack by appointing reliable tribesmen as 'news-agents'. Some were elderly shaikhs and townsmen who simply used children to provide them with information; others daring youngsters and tribal leaders who took great risk in making journeys into enemy-occupied regions. One hot day in June a Canal guard witnessed a scene which said much for Birkil's reputation among the Arabs. The story was told several years later by G. W. Murray:

... two boys, one perhaps seven years of age, the other younger, arrived at the 'bridge-head' post of El-Kubri on the Suez Canal, having walked from 'Ain Sudr thirty-six long desert miles without water. They explained that they were orphans, who had been staying with a Bedouin family there, and that when the food had run short, they had been turned out and told to 'get their food from the English'. Unaware that they had accomplished a feat well beyond the powers of the infantry on the Canal at the time, they asked for Birkil Bey, and broke down and wept when they learnt that he was not immediately accessible. Fortunately we were able to hand them over to him within an hour.[3]

Diary: Sinai Intelligence Accounts to July 1915 [£10 Turkish = £1 English]

11.1.15	Messenger to Yanbo (1)	1.000
1.2.15	To 3 men for work at Aqaba with Capt. Stirling	1.500
19.2.15	To Père Jaussen for expenses in connection with Red Sea Patrol. Pd. ACP	3.000
19.2.15	To Abu Gadail for flour and rice for work on patrol. To Father Jaussen.	2.370
19.2.15	To Salem Id Firdan of Gemsa, to go to Wejh with his Katira. Pd ACP	1.000

22.2.15 Four camels, two days with expedition to Um Bogma. Pd ACP	.960
22.2.15 Man to go along wire from Suez to Abu Zenima. Pd. APC	.200
20.2.15 To Father Jaussen on account of expenses on patrol. Pd. ACP	5.000
Total	15.030

[These amounts were obviously disbursed during the attack on Suez and in the Tor and Abu Zenima engagements.]

28.2.15 Paid to ACP for settlement of above account	.030
20.2.15 To Abu Gadail for goods supplied to Father Jaussen (1)	1.210
27.2.15 Expenses in passing Sayid Muhammad al Idrisi through Suez (2)	1.160
28.2.15 Paid on loan to Zaidan Medakhal	5.000
4.3.15 Paid by Père Jaussen: trip to Suleiman al Rabaia	(.600)
4.3.15 Paid by Père Jaussen to Rabaia abu Darwish	(.600)
4.3.15 Expended by Jaussen on various items not specified during trip on *Desaix*	(3.720)
(Jaussen states he still has £3.080E)	
9.3.15 Issued to Père Jaussen on account	7.00
10.3.15 For Arab clothing for Père Jaussen (3)	1.20
10.3.15 Stores for Father Jaussen to Port Tewfiq	.200
18.3.15 Stores for Capt. Anderson to Port Tewfiq	.100
28.3.15 Stores for Capt. Anderson to Abu Gadail	6.480
28.3.15 Stores for Father Jaussen to Abu Gadail	10.000
7.5.15 One sack flour for Suleiman Bey. Pd. ACP	1.650
7.5.15 One sack dura for Father Jaussen. Pd. ACP	1.150
26.5.15 Pd. by Mr MacMichael[4] to Muhammad Mendil	1.500
4.6.15 For shirts for presents to Arabs. Pd. ACP	1.400
5.7.15 Pd. for Suleiman Bey Muhammad of Billi Safaja, given him by coastguards at Safaja	3.730
(300pt, 42pt, 31pt telegram)	
Rcd. from Intelligence	15.000
Repaid by Zaidan Mudakhil	5.000
Rcd. from DMI	20.000
Returned 10pt (ten pounds Turkish) overpaid to GC	
(Gilbert Clayton, DMI)	

Some interesting facts emerge from this meticulous and mundane record of petty cash expenditure. Sayid Idrisi, the mercurial

African whose family ruled the province of Asir between the Hijaz and Yemen on the Red Sea coast, was persuaded to sign a treaty with the Indian Government in April 1915. It would seem that he made a journey to Cairo in February, probably to negotiate that treaty. He was the bitter enemy of the Imam Yahya of Yemen, and an equivocal ally of Britain. In March 1917 the Resident at Aden agreed to pay him £7,000 a month provided he fought the Turks rather than a private war against the Imam, a stipulation which he studiously ignored.[5]

Father Jaussen appears to have been extremely busy at this time, especially among the tribal leaders in Upper Egypt, the Hijaz and Sinai. He was presumably working for both British and French intelligence since he was conveyed by the French warship *Desaix* between Port Said and the Red Sea. The activities of Intelligence in Sinai, Upper Egypt and the Red Sea area in 1915 become clear from instructions to agents recorded in Parker's diary from April of that year.

Auda Salama and *Sanad Salama* [brothers]: to watch Hajj road, al-Towil, Um al Saihera and Al Giddi [territory NE of Suez in *dira* of Lahweitat tribe]. Pay £1 [English] per month, and more for anything they bring. Appointed 9.4.15. Paid £2E for intelligence 29.4.15. To go out at once 4.5.15.

Salama Awad and *Ayad Salman*: to remain near Ain Sudr and report. Pay £1E per month and more for information. Appointed 10.4.15. Advanced £1E each. Paid £2E for intelligence. To go out at once 4.5.15. Paid £50 [Turkish] 17.5.15.

Salman Obaidallah [Lahaiwat tribe]: To go to Nakhl and return. Payment by results [no date]. Paid in advance £50T.

Auda Salem ibn Ayad [Dubur]: to go to Nakhl to ask where Auda Musleh is. To pay particular attention to aeroplanes and horses. Also Arabs at Nakhl and of course numbers of troops. 11.4.15 Paid £150T, 24.4.15. Paid £100T 5.5.15 to stay at Sudr for 15 days and return.

Ayad ibn Sai'id [Hamadha – an inferior tribe said to descend from original inhabitants of Sinai]: given wire and tools to repair [telegraph] wire as far as Gharandil. Promised 15 pounds (T) per day for three men (self and two others) for reasonable time and an extra £1E if line works. And if line works for seven days to receive £5E and no daily pay. Left Ayun Musa 11.4.15. Advanced by Haj Ismail £75T worth grain etc. (Companions Hamud Abu Rizh and Salman Salama.) Paid £2E for intelligence 29.4.15. Paid £15T (3 men for five days) and £1E reward for work on telegraph.

Ali Suleiman [Howaitat]: to cross [canal] at Kubri and go to Um Mukhshaib, Hegayib, Rodh Salem, Hamra, Maghara and return. Expected in ten days. Payment by results. 11 April 1915.

Ayad Salem [western Howaitat]: to go to Towal and thence to eastern edge of Raha [hills] and patrol from Sudr to Bir al Ramh for 4 days. If nothing happens to go to Rodh Salem and vicinity and return. Pay by results. 12.4.15.

Auda Musleh [Howaitat]: told off to remain at Towal and watch, and Sudr al Heitan, and Wadi Um Saihera. Promised reward for news. Appointed 14.4.15. Paid £2E for intelligence 29.4.15. To go out again at once 4.5.15.

Ayad Salem: told to go with brother Awad and remain at al Fogeia or Yurga and give immediate news of any movement on Abu Zenima and Tor from Nakhl. Pay at £1E month for each, and payment by results. Paid £1E advance and £1E for report 4.5.15.

Musa Abu Talheiza: to go to Fogeia to find out about Awarma [subdivision of Towara], returning in ten days. Advanced £20T. Paid £80T, remainder of month's pay, 3.6.15. Paid £1E, 7.5.15.

Deifalla Suleiman: to cross to Ayun Musa and make detour round Mabeyuk and Nawatla and report to any post, paying special attention to tracks of camels, horses or mules, and numbers also of guns or anything heavy. Appointed 28.4.15. Paid £1E, 7.5.15.

Salman Ayad Abu Talheiza: ditto, but sleeping at Ayun Musa and leaving there tomorrow morning. Appointed 28.4.15. Paid £1E, 7.5.15.

Faraj Salam [Badara – a small tribe of about twenty tents at Jabal Ejma; regarded by Arab tribes as 'Ajam' or non-Arab]: to remain at Ain Yurga at £1E per month from 20.5.15 and give news of any move towards Tor or Abu Zenima. News paid for in addition.

Sanad Salama: Sent out 4.5.15. Came in 25.5.15. No news. Paid £1E for first month to 8.5.15.

Auda Salama: Paid £50T, 6.5.15. Paid £1E for first month to 8.5.15.

Auda Musleh: came in 26.5.15. To take up residence at Um Mukshaib. Paid £1E first month's pay to 13.5.15.

Auda Salem ibn Ayad: Paid one month to 23.5.15. Sent £10T to get information as to who attended meeting on 1st Ragab [April] at Nakhl, especially as to Aleiqat and Muzeina [tribesmen]. 20.7.15 sent to Ain Sudr via Mabeyuk and Wadi Raha returning via Wadi Sudr. paid £1E.

Salama Salam [Lahaiwat]: to Ayaba via Thamad and Nakhl with Silmi Musalam. News brought little and indifferent. Paid for trip of 15 days, £150T. Living at Suez. June 9, 1915 to go to Abu Jarad, Haleifia and thence to Somar and Ain Sudr and back to get news of Posts and Awarma especially. Pd. £20T. Returns 14 June. No news except that he was not allowed to go on by post at Haleifia. Paid another £30T.

Salama Awad: sent out 1.6.15. Advanced pay to 10.6.15, £1E. Paid £50T for Suleiman Abu Aliyan of Turabin [Towara tribe], whom he is going to employ, 7.6.15. Pd. £100T and ordered to Nakhl for news, 15.7.15.

Ayad Salman: to accompany above. Advanced pay to 10.6.15. £1E, 1.6.15.

Musa Abu Talheiza: Came in July lst with little news. Sent out and paid £50T, 19.7.15. Comes back with story of army at Ain Sudr. Afraid to go out again. Not worth employing.

Ayad Salem: sent out on 18th to find truth of story of army at Sudr. Returns 22nd. Information apparently good. Paid £1E, 22.7.15.

Sabai'il Suleiman (Hamadha): 20.7.15. Sent out via Mabeyuk to Ain Sudr, via Wadi Raha, returning via W. Sudr, Abu Jarad, Abu Kataif to Ain Musa. Pd. £70T.

Some of the activity at this time east of Suez was designed to catch one Shablaq, a shaikh of the Howaitat who was a known enemy spy. Eventually another leader of that tribe, Saad abu Nar, was held hostage at Suez until Shablaq surrendered.[6]

If remuneration for Parker's spies in Sinai was not princely, it was sufficient by the standards of desert society in 1915 to tempt a few tribesmen (who would doubtless have served either side for a few shillings) to risk life and limb. By following their movements in the months following the first attack on the Canal we can see that Intelligence cast its net mainly along a narrow grid from far north to far south, but seldom further inland from Suez than the 75 miles (120 km) to Nakhl. In fact, Maxwell had decided that Sinai could not be defended at its frontier. Only the immediate vicinity of the Canal on its east bank and the coastal region to Tor would be garrisoned. From late February 1915 all eyes were turned across the Mediterranean to the Dardanelles. If Jamal's army had reformed at Beersheba, Maxwell's Staff was entirely preoccupied with the battle of the Constantinople Straits which Churchill and Lloyd George had advocated, Kitchener had acceded to, and Fisher the First Sea Lord had opposed to the point of resignation. Parker was left almost alone to keep watch on Sinai. But as the Dardanelles campaign reached its terrible climax of military and naval disaster in the summer of 1915, the army commander, Gen. Ian Hamilton, turned to Cairo with a request that it should renew the effort to bring about an Arab rebellion and thus weaken the Turkish army by forcing it to fight on other fronts. In October the diary records 'Notes. Arab Tribes in Arabia'. The information on which his summary is based seems to have come from Lawrence, who had been working at this time with Hogarth on the preparation of a 'Blue Book' on the tribes, to which Gertrude Bell would become the most informed contributor when she appeared in Cairo at the end of the year. For the moment, however, Lawrence was putting his pre-war travels in Syria and Mesopotamia to good use, while Hogarth added the information supplied through the War Office in London, the Indian Army Intelligence Department and the Royal Geographical Society in London, by the two most informed travellers in those regions, Shakespear and Leachman.

Parker was in close touch with Father Jaussen during the 'Dardanelles' months. In August 1915 he received a report from that remarkable priest headed: *Pour l'usage personnel du Colonel Parker et du Major Newcombe. Disparation des deux matelots anglais.* In reporting the strange affair of the missing sailors off the Hijaz coast he delivered a mild broadside on the subject of Britain's interrogation techniques.

On 20 July, at about midday, HMS *Hardinge* was patrolling in the region of the island of Um Sahra [off Um Lejj] when it apprehended an Arab craft and ordered it to approach. The order was refused and the ship's commander sent two armed sailors to board the Arab craft and bring it alongside. By 5.30 in the afternoon the craft had mysteriously disappeared. It never came alongside. That is all. I did not know the number of people on the craft. I was given different accounts, five, eight and thirteen, men and children. On the 21st the *Hardinge* had no news of the Arab craft of the missing English sailors. No more has since come to light.

It was a strange affair indeed. It may be that *Hardinge* was engaged in an activity with far-reaching aims, and that Jaussen's presence aboard was an embarrassment to naval intelligence officers. They would probably not have known that he was working for Parker, and perhaps assumed that he was a French agent. At any rate, the agent-priest went on:

On board *Hardinge* there appeared a child of about ten years who said under interrogation that he had seen the boat and that the two English matelots were taken from it. I was not able to see this child or to interrogate him because he was sent away by the Commander along with his elder brother before I could get to him. However, another of his brothers, Mahmud Hamdan, was kept as a prisoner on the *Hardinge*. He was interrogated by two interpreters, who wanted to hear from him confirmation of his brother's story. They took the child aside, placed his hand on the Koran, made him swear to tell the truth, and one of the interpreters stood before him, baton in hand, in order to scare him. The young Mahmud, terrified, confessed that like his youngest brother he had seen the boat, with two men dressed in white aboard it.

I learnt of this not from the interpreters or the Commander but from an Arab soldier aboard, Ibrahim Hassan. Straight away I had Mahmud brought to me and being no longer in a state of terror he assured me that he had lied to the interpreters in order to avoid a beating. He told me that he had not seen the boat, nor in consequence had he seen the English sailors. The child had witnessed nothing. Would his younger brother's testimony be any better?

I relate this story not for the malicious satisfaction of contradicting whatever it was that happened, but to show that information obtained by inexperienced interpreters is worthless.

I recall another event to which I was witness. I was asking a Bedouin how many soldiers there were at Dhiba. He answered 'About ten'. An interpreter interrupted. 'That's not true. There are at least 3,000.' The Bedouin readily agreed. In fact he outbid the interpreter. 'More', he said.

To return to our sailors. On 2 August, a Negro called Faraj arrived on board. He was the slave of Rahman Shahatt, and was at Um Lejj on 29 July when the Governor sent out 300 camel riders to look for the English sailors [the Governor at this time was, of course, a Turk]. On their return they claimed that they had heard and seen nothing. It should be pointed out that had they found the sailors they could, at a pinch, have concealed them. The affair, as far as *Hardinge* was concerned, was dealt with entirely by the Commander and an interpreter called Muhammad.

These events took place a year before the Arab Revolt and the entry into the war on the Allied side of the Sharif of Mecca, the servant of the Sultan of the Ottoman Empire. Jaussen told the Arabs of Um Sahra, 'This act will not go unpunished. Blood calls for blood.' He believed that the Arabs on the boarded *sambuq* were tempted by the sight of the handsome firearms of the British, and murdered them as a simple act of piracy. He concluded his report:

This incident gave the English Government an excellent excuse to place a camp of at least 500 men on the nearby island of Hassani. The island is ideally placed at the entrance to a bay offering ample anchorage for ships. At the eastern side is a plain, about three or four km. perhaps, on the edge of which, at the coast, is the palmed village of the Alat tribe which spends part of the winter on the island (not the summer as the Naval manual says). On the western side, the island terminates in a hill about 180–200 metres high. . . . I was on the beach one evening and was struck by the cool freshness of the wind blowing from the west. Even in summer the heat does not seem unbearable.

And then:

Bearing in mind the important position of Um Lejj, occupying the island of Hassani could be of immense advantage in observing and influencing Arabia. Of course one could take advantage of a military occupation to place storehouses on the island. The policy of gentle handling and friendliness towards the Arabs seems to give excellent results and should be continued, while reserving the right to punish pirates.

Just before the rebellion of the Sharif of Mecca in June 1916, the Royal Navy would make Hassani Island its principal base off the western coast of Arabia.

The notes on the tribes were marked 'T.E.L.' and their style suggests the hand of the *enfant terrible* of the Savoy Hotel, though they are in Parker's writing.

Notes: October 1915 T. E. L.: Arab Tribes in Arabia

Shammar: not a Confederation, but a huge mass of hardly-related tribes of the same name. The greatest man is of course Ibn Rashid of Hail, but for the immediate present we are more likely to come into touch with the *Shammar-Jerba*, or the *Shammar Toqa*.

The Shammar-Jerba: split into two feuds, under chiefs of a Muwalli family: the quarrel began some generations back, and is unlikely to close up. (1) under the children of Farhan (Al Asi and brother) live in Tigris valley. Wander north of Diarbakr and south of Baghdad, and westward to Deir az–Zor [known as Awlad Farhan]. Very religious and have noted 'Turkizing' tendency, which is cause of quarrel with other branch led by the children of Abdal Karim [Awlad Abdal Karim] who are Abdal Mehsin and Muhammad; (2) wander all over central Mesopotamia as far north as Kurds, Circassians and Yezidis of Ras al Ain and the Sinjar will let them, as far south as Hail, and as far west as the Anaiza will let them. Principal tribes – the Faddagha and Sinjara. Abdal Karim was hanged by the Turks, with connivance of brother Farhan, and the active assistance of the Muntafiq. In consequence his descendants are always at war with the Muntafiq, and bickering with their cousins, the children of Farhan. In addition they have to maintain their old hostility with the Anaiza. They also fight with some Kurd tribes. In consequence of all this the Shammar Jerba are somewhat overtaxed, and are not as powerful as they were. The relations of the Jerba with Ibn Rashid are interesting. They helped him with a contingent when he marched against Ibn Saud in the spring of 1915 [the battle of Jarab in which Shakespear was killed]: and they look upon the hail Amirate as a great credit to their name and family: but on account of their more pressing home enmities, and the fear of the Anaiza, they are never able to afford him any assistance of importance.

The Shammar Toqa: agriculturalists in the neighbourhood of Baghdad. They are a 'meskin' people.

The Shammar of Najd: belong mainly to the Sinjara, Abda and Aslam. Ibn Rashid is so much their Amir that the sub-shaikhs have little place and influence. The majority of the semi-settled people of Jabal Shammar are Bani Temim. Ibn Rashid has always been pro-Turkish: there have been continual intrigues between him and the Turks, and they have helped him with men on two occasions, and have given him guns and rifles quite recently (they are old guns of course). He has always been suspicious of foreign influence, and though not at all fanatical, is unlikely to touch us, as we are tainted by our relations with Ibn Saoud. ('Ibn Rahid' is used generally of the family: there is a rumour current that the Amir is now one of the elder uncles: possibly a new murder has taken place.)

The Anaiza: not so numerous probably as the Harb, or the Shammar, but are very rich, and have politically minded chiefs. They also occupy a peculiar strategic position: All up the East fringe of Syria, out to Jauf, and down the West edge of Mesopotamia. This makes them, for us, much more important than the inland Harb, and as important as the Shammar. They came into the Hamad [Syrian desert] about 1750, and drove the Shammar across the Euphrates into Mesopotamia. Their beat goes from Aleppo-Meskene area to Ana and Hit, southwest to Jauf, and thence down the Haj road near Taima. They are the people principally to be reckoned with in connecting the Hijaz with Syria (as the tribes between them and the coast, the Billi, Amran, Auf, Howaitat, Zobaid, are weak and divided), and at present being hostile to Ibn Rashid, and occupying the whole of Wadi Sirhan and Jauf, they cut him off entirely from Damascus. Their main strength used to be in the Hauran, but they have been turned out by the Circassians and the Druzes, with both of which they are on bad terms. Their hereditary enemies are the Shammar, with whom they fight continually. They eke out their time fighting among themselves. The Ruwalla and the Bishr were bickering two years ago.

The principal sub-tribes of the Anaiza are in order of size:

(i) The Wuld Ali: More a confederation than a tribe: have very many branches, totalling perhaps 8,000 tents: many of them Anaiza not by blood but by alliance. Their beat runs from Homs to Taima (which belongs to the Wuld Suleiman, a subtribe of the Wuld Ali) and their principal men are: Rashid ibn Smeyr (Hauran), Muhammad ibn Saleh al Tayar, Saoud ibn Milhem (Homs)

The *Bani Sakhr* depend on the Wuld Ali, though not blood relations, and are under Ibn Smeyr. Their biggest man is Fawaz ibn Faiz.

(ii) The Amarat: very far South East. They are from Meshed and Ana on the Lower Euphrates, and in winter go into Najd. They have many subdivisions. Their chief shaikh (who is perhaps the weightiest man in the whole Anaiza confederation) is Fahd ibn Abdal Mehsin Dugheim ibn Hadhdhal.

(iii)The Bishr: a name for the confederation of the Sebaa and the Fidan. They are the northernmost of the Anaiza, and are about Aleppo, Deir [az-Zor], and Hama. Chief Shaikhs of Sebaa are Ghithwan ibn Murshid, and Burjeus ibn Hadeib. The Fidan are stronger. They are split into the Dhana Kuheil, Shaikh Hashim ibn Mehaid; and the

Supervising the first Sinai boundary pillar at Taba near Aqaba, 1906.

Mount Sinai, Jabal Musa, from the plain of Raha. Jabal Sufsafa (Horeb of bible) on left.

The Convent of St Catherine.

Turquoise mines at Um Bogma near Abu Zanima, photographed by German travellers in about 1906. Governor's tent in valley. The ore from these hills is recovered by grubbing; 'mines' only by courtesy.

Winifred Parker halts on the road to Nakhl.

Winifred's camel train arrives at the fortress of Nakhl, November 1909, complete with piano and sofa.

Winifred on camel 'Gaisan' at Nakhl.

The crescent flag, emblem of formal Ottoman sovereignty in Egypt, flies over the quarantine station at Tor, 1910.

Pilgrims at Tor, 1910.

Shaikh Musa Nasir, chief of the Towara (southern
tribes), 1910.

Shaikh Mudakhil Suleiman.

Zaidan, son of Mudakhil.

Salama, Wallier's *shikari* in 1906 and one of his principal
agents in war.

Sudanese police and Egyptian *mudir* at Kuntilla frontier post, photographed by Capt. W.H.I. Shakespear, 1914. Royal Geographical Society.

Sudanese police at al-Arish, 1909, with *mudir* Muhammad Tewfiq Khairi.

Parker with Dr Sterling, head of the Christian Mission School at Gaza, 1910.

Captain L.B. Weldon, 'intelligence' colleague in war, at Gaza 1910.

Dhana Mejid, Shaikh Hashim ibn Gayshish. Hashim ibn Mehaid takes the lead of the whole Bishr in any crisis. He is a fighting man, but clever, and a gentleman.

(iv) The Ruwalla: with the Mahalaf are called Jelaas. They live about Damascus and have huge masses of camels and some horses. From their position they are more in the public eye than any other Anaiza tribe, and, thanks to Nuri Shalan, their biggest shaikh, and a politician, they have considerable weight with the Turkish Government in Damascus. Nuri is the most politically minded of any Anaiza shaikh (Hashim second, Ibn Hadhal third) [the Arabic 'shaddah' or doubled consonant in this and other names is unnecessary in English and I have generally dropped it from here on], and very influential.

   He is not a very attractive person, and is probably rather crooked in his ways.

The people worth buying in this lot are from our point of view:
(I) Nuri Shalan, owner of Jof [Jauf], and controller of the Haj Railway line.
(II) Hachim ibn Mehaid, who controls the Euphrates line of communication as far north as Jarablus
(III) Ibn Hadhal, who is a buffer between Baghdad and Hail.

Other large Arab Tribes

The Harb: are in two great branches, the Bani Salem, and the Bani Ali. One half of them follow Ibn Rashid and half obey the Sharif of Mecca, since Rashid lost reputation. They are very clanish, and hard fighters: many of them are semi-nomadic. If they united they would probably be the most numerous of all the tribes, but they have an inland position only, and concern the inland politics of Arabia. They are nearly without horses. Chief shaikhs are Ghati ibn Neheith (Bani Salem) and Mehsin al Ithm (Bani Ali). Their beat is roughly from the Hijaz to Hail and south to Riyadh.

The Ataiba: are composed of the main branches Roqa and Barqa (Shaikh Turki ibn Maslat, and Muhammad ibn Haidi). They used to belong to Ibn Saoud, but the Wahhabi manners offended them, and they recently 'verted to the Sharif'. They live east of Wadi Rumma, and near Mecca and Taif. They have many sheep, camels and horses, and have a great fighting reputation. They are old enemies of the Harb, and about half as numerous.

The Dhuffir: live in north-east Najd about Zobair and Samawa. Their greatest shaikh is Hamad ibn Suwait. Not very large in numbers.

The Muntafiq: a confederation made out of some of the Ajwad, Bani Temim, and Bani Saad by the Sadun family. Ajaimi is now leading Shaikh. They are Shi'ite and have large flocks and herds, and many of them live in villages. They used to fight the Turks continually, till the latter recognized their shaikh as Governor of the Province, and since then they have been more contented, but there are many old grudges between them. Ajaimi is now helping the Turks as much as he can against us. They are very numerous indeed.

Bani Lam: live along the Tigris about Amara and Ali Gharbi: many are sedentary. Shaikhs are Lazem, Benaia, Ghadban and Musa. Some of them are helping us actively.

The semi-nomad and semi-sedentary tribes are far larger in numbers than the true nomads. The Muntafiq alone are probably as large as all the Anaiza: though they have about one-tenth the reputation.

These tribal notes, betraying in their style and even in their punctuation, a distinctive dash of T. E. Lawrence, embrace interesting asides. The references to the Rashid of Hail, for example, show a distinctly hazy understanding of the attitude of the Amir Saud ibn Rashid and his Chief Minister Saud ibn Saleh towards the Turks at this time, October 1915. Saud ibn Rashid, described elsewhere in British intelligence files as a 'jungle youth' was not so much a political intriguer as a simple-minded and boorish young man whose only interest in life, according to Leachman, who camped with him in 1910, was horsemanship. Both Britain and Turkey despaired of him as a potential ally. He had certainly not been deposed or murdered, and he ruled until 1920 when he became the last reigning victim of his homicidal family. But if the intelligence files composed by Hogarth and his team in Cairo were not always accurate, they were clear in the intentions they revealed. 'The people worth buying in this lot . . .',

suggested an early awareness of strategic problems in Mesopotamia (where British and Indian troops were on the verge of
disaster after their initial successes) and the Hijaz where military
operations were obviously foreseen despite the fact that Britain's
negotiations with the Sharif of the holy cities were far from
concluded, and the Sharif and his sons were in close communion
with the Turkish authorities.[7] In the hiatus of 1915, Col. Parker
and Father Jaussen had each made several journeys by sea to the
Hijaz coast in search of agents, but they had had little success.

An intriguing postscript to the tribal detail copied into the
diary in October 1915, was a list of Pan-Arabs, some of whom
were already in touch with the High Commissioner in Cairo in
connection with the negotiations with the Sharif of Mecca, and
most of whom had been members of the Committees which had
promulgated the earlier plan of rebellion.

Ali Rida Rikabi of Aleppo. Was Civil Governor of Lebanon. Not
religious. Very rich.

Izzat Pasha. Formerly Private Secretary to Abdal Hamid (Sultan of
Turkey). Of Damascus. When Pan-Arab movement nearly became
rebellion was to be king of Damascus. Old. Intriguer. Not religious.
Unsafe.

Rashid Riza. Damascus. Leans towards Pan-Islamism.

Hashim ibn Mehaid. Shaikh of Bishr-Anaiza. Anti-Turk. Pan-Arab
Society of Sharif al Faruqi. Under influence of Madame Koch of
Aleppo, she being in pay of Baron von Oppenheim (chief of German
Foreign Office Eastern Bureau).

Four sons of Ibrahim Pasha (deceased) of Milli Kurds. East of Urfa. Two
sons now fighting against Russians. Khalil is most important son. HQ
Rakka. Pro-Arab. Well known by Sykes.

Baghdad. Al Asi and Ibn Farhan, sons of Abdal Karim, who was hanged
by Turks. Of the Jerba-Shammar.

Nuri Shalan. Shaikh of Ruwalla Anaiza. Not religious. Conquered Jof
(Jauf) and gave it to his son. Very rich and powerful. Member of every

Arab League. Civilized and townified. On good terms with Turkish Government.[8]

Sharif al Faruqi. Townsman of Mosul. Rich. Good descent.

Shukri Pasha. Strong Pan-Arab. Probably religious. Aleppine. Rashid Riza looks up to him. Was in command at Adana and perhaps a depot commander now.

These notes again bear the stamp, and the initials, of Lawrence. They lend some credence to the belief that T. E. L's intelligence activities between 1911 and 1914, when he was officially working as an archaeologist at Jerablus (Carchemish), were more clandestine than was previously thought to be the case. Recent research in the French General Staff records at Vincennes,[9] reveals that Lawrence was a member of 'a certain' Damascus Committee. The inclusion of the name 'Sharif Faruqi' in this list suggests that Lawrence had inside knowledge, since Faruqi did not desert to the British lines at Gallipoli until late October and did not arrive in Cairo until the end of the month, when he told interrogators that he was a leading member of Al Ahad, and that its civil counterpart, Al Fatah, had its headquarters in London and that 'not all its members were Arab'. Faruqi also said that he had met the Sharif's son Faisal at Aleppo in April 1915. He was enrolled in British intelligence, given the code identification 'G' and sent as secret messenger to the Sharif. It was the French Deuxieme Bureau which betrayed the committee members still in Syria to the Turks by leaving documents at the Beirut consulate at the outbreak of war.[10] Most of them were hanged by Jamal in 1916. Newcombe, Maitland, Murphy, Bray and Leachman, among Cairo and Indian Staff officers, and the Political Agent Shakespear, all had contact with the Damascus and Baghdad Committees from 1911. There is circumstantial evidence that Lawrence, and perhaps his colleagues Woolley and Campbell-Thompson, may have been covert members of the civilian 'Fatah'. It is unlikely that they would have been admitted to the military 'Covenant', al Ahad.

If Parker knew little about the tribes of Arabia proper, he was probably the greatest living expert on those of Sinai and the northern Hijaz. The rudimentary notes for Hogarth's *Blue Book*, which Gertrude Bell would update from the moment of her arrival in Cairo as a recruit to Clayton's intelligence office in November 1915, were doubtless intended to assist Parker in the pursuit of the plan to cause an uprising among the Arab Tribes of which the new High Commissioner in Cairo, Sir Henry McMahon, had taken charge; a plan which, if it came off, would involve all the great shaikhs of the peninsula one way or another. For the moment he was concerned to make contact with the west-coast shaikhs of Arabia in order to test out their loyalties should an Allied invasion of the Red Sea area become necessary, or an alliance with the Sharif be cemented. Soon after the February attack on Suez, a party of French marines had landed at Aqaba and the small Turkish garrison took to its heels. An invasion of that part of the northern Hijaz coast by Sudanese troops able to withstand the intense summer heat was one obvious possibility as a back up to any Arab uprising.

In late December 1914 Parker had made a tour of the main ports of the Hijaz aboard the *Northbrook*, going ashore in rowing-boats, usually at dusk or dawn, with trustworthy Arabs. On 25 December he had reported to Clayton details of tribal attitudes and rifts, and Turkish garrisons.

Muwailah and Dhiba: Both ports are in the country of the Howaitat (Shaikh Ahmad Muhammad abu Dikaka). The shaikh was appointed last year ... At Dhiba there are said to be eight soldiers in the tower but all the inhabitants have gone inland, frightened of warships. At Muwailah there are said to be two watchmen and a certain Husain abu Saluja, but all the people have gone to the hills. Possibly Shaikh Hassan ibn Gad's people [Howaitat] also use Muwailah as a port from the north, and Amran of Saleh ibn Makbal.

Bida: North of Muwailah, belongs to Musaid under Muhammad al Tarfawi.

Al Shureih, Hakal, Al Hamaida: Are all Amran places, up as far as Aqaba. Amran Shaikhs, Salim ibn Makbal and Helaiyl ibn Kasim al Asabin.

Latter said to be more intelligent.

Aqaba: In addition to Amran at Aqaba there are also Howaitat [Alawin] under Hassan ibn Muhammad ibn Gad. Hassan's uncle, Ali ibn Husain [no relation to son of Sharif of Mecca of same name] is more intelligent.

Al Wejh: Chief man is Suleiman Pasha abu Rifada [Billi tribe]. He is at loggerheads with a certain Hamid, whose father was shaikh before Suleiman Pasha. Latter gives Hamid no share of dues, which he resents. Suleiman helped to supplant Aliyan abu Dikaka and presumably has power at Muwailah and Dhiba. The Billi and Maaza used to be at war with Howaitat but at present there is peace. Said to be a garrison, strength unknown.

Yanbo: Said to be no garrison, but unlikely as this is the port of Madina. All the people, except those too old and weak, are said to have left. Yanbo and the country south as far as Jiddah is probably inhabited by Harb and Juhaina tribes.

Um Lejj: Port of this name unmarked on maps, but is mentioned as a port by informant.

The diary entry for 29 December gives a succinct picture of Arabian coastal reconnaissance in the first weeks of war:

Approached shore again at Al Wejh, numbers of camels and women and men left town for the hills on seeing the ship. About 10.30 a.m. Two small sambuks were seen south of reef which runs out eastwards from Reikha island. Six men, wading and in two small boats, landed on island. Galley was sent to island and interpreter landed to try and get touch. Meantime they apparently made off to a tiny island SE. Interpreter found no one. Galley returned to ship at 12.10. At 1.30 p.m. neared town, men visible on roofs of houses near mosque dressed in white mostly. Ship proceeded north slowly . . . Two men seen to be proceeding along path northwards but too far inland for it to be possible to intercept them as messengers. Galley was sent with unarmed crew to put up flag on beach, with a letter, about 1 ½ miles north of town. Galley was about 400 yards from beach when ten or twelve Arabs with rifles began advancing over crest of low hills towards beach. These were followed by another eight or so and a Turk apparently – 15 men or so came skirmishing northwards from town . . . Galley recalled and hoisted from about 300 yards from beach. Ship proceeded to sea. More men then seen returning to town, among them six (apparently) Turks.

On 6 January 1915 Parker sent a coded telegram [dated 5 January] to the DMI from Tor, recounting the surveillance exercise in the Red Sea. He also sent Clayton copies of correspondence with the shaikhs of the coastal ports conducted during a voyage in the following week.

15 January 1915: to Clayton, War Office, Cairo: Telegram 131
Recent tour in *Northbrook* shows that it is impossible to communicate with Arabs in Hijaz from a warship. It had been hoped to find a *sambuk* and send her in with message but no success. At Wejh fishermen on an adjacent island fled when approached and later inhabitants of town together with a few Turks prepared to attack apparently unarmed boat on its near shore. I suggest possibly satisfactory method of getting in touch with Wejh, Dhiba and Muwailah is by trustworthy messengers from Ibrahim abu Gadail to Howaitat and Billi shaikhs proceeding by *sambuk* to trade at those places.

On 6 January Parker sent a coded telegram to the DMI from Tor, recounting the surveillance work of the past month in the Red Sea. He also sent Clayton copies of correspondence with the shaikhs of the coastal towns conducted during the recent voyage.

11 January 1915 (and Arabic date). (Telegrams translation)
To the Sharif Ghalib, Amir of Arabs of Yanbo and district
After greetings – I write to make known to you that there is no enmity between the English and the Arabs; of this you are no doubt already aware. Nevertheless, all trade appears to have been entirely broken off between the Hijaz and Egypt, and I think this is perhaps because you think we are making war on you. And the consequence is that all grain has risen much in price, greatly to the distress of the poor. I therefore suggest you should meet me so that I may explain how trade may possibly be reopened between Egypt and the Hijaz, since we are not at

war. And if you will meet me please send a reply immediately as to the time and place that will suit you, and I shall be obliged if you can meet me this day.

> With respects,
> A. C. Parker, Former Governor, Sinai

To Commandant of Ship for Parker Bey
I have received your letter in which you say there is no enmity between the English and the Arabs. This is not the case, since there is a deep-seated enmity and previously there have been no dealings, except officially. And since you have made war on our Sultan, the Commander of the Faithful, and made war on God and on his Prophet, all with the intention of destroying our religion, the true one, we cannot deal with you; and you are attacking the Commander of the Faithful and our brother Muhammadans. And therefore soon, with God and his Prophet to help us, we shall free our brother Muhammadans, the inhabitants of Egypt, from the tyranny and slavery of your hands, and the flag of the Prophet shall fly over all her boundaries [Egypt], and over all the Muhammadan world. And we are not in need of any trade or provisions from you. God will provide for us. And we shall have sufficient for five years. And we, the inhabitants of the Hijaz, children of God's Prophet, have been ready at all times to wage war on you. And shortly we shall meet you in Egypt and will expel you thence, as our fathers and ancestors before expelled you. From God the victory and the possession soon. Give warning to all Muslims O Muhammad. But if you will turn to Muhammadism, that will be better for you. Salaam.

> Amir of Arabs of Yanbo and district,
> Al Sharif Muhammad Ali

Parker had been misled by his messengers and had written to the wrong man. Ghalib was the brother of the Amir, Muhammad Ali. Later the same day he replied to Muhammad Ali, with an emphatic essay on the origin of the war.

I have received your letter, and without taking exception to its abruptness, I beg to inform you that it is the Germans who have dragged the Turkish Empire into this war by trickery and deceit, and the way they did it was by taking the warships of Turkey and firing on Russian towns and ships, and this without the permission or wish of the Sultan. Thus they drew Turkey into a war with France, England and Russia without any of the latter having made any hostile move. . . .

On 14 January Parker reported again to the DMI, Cairo. He described the latest efforts to make contact with Arab leaders along the Red Sea coast, and admitted that all his communications had been 'unsatisfactory'. As for the Amir of Yanbo, he told Clayton: 'The messenger was desired to hand the letter himself to the Arab Governor, whose name he said was the Sharif Ghalib. As appears in the reply, this was not his name; nor did the messenger hand in the letter personally. It is quite likely therefore that the reply was inspired by the Turkish officer commanding the garrison, which consisted, according to the old fisherman, of about a hundred men.' [His telegram ended:] 'It appears difficult to establish any kind of friendly intercourse with the Arabs of Hijaz.'

In August he was called to GHQ Cairo, and in October he went to the War Office in London, to help Col. B. T. Buckley at MO2 who was then dealing with the Ottoman Empire and its Arab territories, and trying to make sense of the Sharifian negotiations which Kitchener had set in motion a year before.

It was a tremulous Whitehall and a disjointed General Staff to which Parker reported in October 1915. The mounting disasters of the Dardanelles campaign wracked the ministers who had pushed for it and divided the generals and admirals who, whether they liked it or not, were saddled with its execution. Five months earlier Fisher, the First Sea Lord, had brought down the Asquith Government by resigning his post. In the new coalition, Kitchener remained Secretary of State for War; but the man who had once dominated affairs from his office on the first floor, with a CIGS [11] next door who trembled at the sight of him, and a War Cabinet across the road which dared not dispute his word, was a broken figure. If the Dardanelles had been primarily Churchill's brain-child – he was peremptorily dismissed from his Admiralty post in May 1915 – Kitchener had gone along with it, and had begun to pay the price of a defeat which though not yet conceded was inevitable. But politicians and some generals began to see a prospect of rescuing something from the wreckage in the shape of an Arab Revolt, led by the Sharif Husain of Mecca, at the heart of the Ottoman dominions. Sir Ian Hamilton had pleaded with High Commissioner McMahon at the time of the Gallipoli landings to precipitate such a rebellion. By September 1915 negotiations with the Sharif were beginning to bear fruit, though the wily Husain's price was high. The affair which Kitchener's note to the Sharif's son Abdullah had set in motion in September 1914, had by now become the direct responsibility of the Foreign Office and the High Commissioner in Cairo. The War Office was virtually a bystander. But Gen. Callwell's Military Operations directorate, for whom Parker and Buckley laboured in room 223, was kept informed of the highly secret negotiations. By the end of the year they were embroiled in a web of international intrigue as France and Russia demanded their share of the Ottoman spoils (in the event of victory, of course). Sir Mark Sykes, a dynamic figure known to Parker from pre-war days in Cairo, became effectively the chief liaison officer between the War and Foreign Offices, and took over with the Frenchman Picot the conduct of Anglo-French affairs in Ottoman territories. In November the War Committee finally decided on a withdrawal from the Dardanelles and Kitchener offered his resignation to Asquith, but even at the lowest ebb of war, such a contingency was unthinkable. The British public would not hear of it. Nevertheless, by the end of 1915 a drastic shake-up in the War Office was inescapable. Sir Archibald Murray, who had briefly taken over from his namesake Wolfe Murray as CIGS, was nominated to succeed Maxwell as GOC-in-Chief, Egypt. Sir William Robertson, the general who had entered the army as a private and would rise uniquely to the rank of Field Marshal, became the new Chief of Staff. And for the first time a directorate of Military Intelligence was established within the General Staff. Gen. Macdonogh, who had been in charge of counter-intelligence (MO5) under Callwell's military operations wing, became the new Director of Military Intelligence. Parker found himself alongside Col. Buckley at the birth of the new directorate, dealing with Turkey and its empire, Egypt and the Sudan. From room 223, where he was employed until January 1916, he was able to observe the painful and humiliating decline in the prestige of his famous, shy and taciturn uncle; to witness the politicians who had forced him into a tactical corner bay for his blood in their search for a convenient scapegoat. He was back in Egypt by that searing day in June 1916 when news came through that Kitchener had been drowned in the sinking of the *Hampshire*. On the same memorable day, the 5th of the month, news came to MI 2 (b) from Cairo that the Sharif had raised the flag of revolt at Mecca. At the start of a turbulent year in London, a year in which the unselective tragedy of war struck his own family and numbed the British public, he had returned to Cairo, to join Britain's military mission to the Sharif. He had applied in vain while in London to be allowed to serve on the Western Front.

5
The Arab Bureau

> We called ourselves 'Intrusive' as a band; for we meant to break
> into the accepted halls of English foreign policy, and build a new
> people in the East, despite the rails laid down for us by our
> ancestors. Therefore from our hybrid intelligence office in Cairo
> . . . we began to work upon all chiefs, far and near. Sir Henry
> McMahon, High Commissioner in Egypt, was, of course, our
> first effort; and his shrewd insight and tried, experienced mind
> understood our design at once and judged it good. Others, like
> Wemyss, Neil Malcolm, Wingate, supported us in their pleasure
> at seeing the war turned constructive. Their advocacy confirmed
> in Lord Kitchener the favourable impression he had derived
> years before when Sharif Abdullah appealed to him in Egypt;
> and so McMahon at last achieved our foundation stone, the
> understanding with the Sharif of Mecca.
>
> T.E. Lawrence, *Seven Pillars of Wisdom*

Of the men who took part in the adventure which Lawrence
described famously, none recorded in detail the inter-office
rivalries of the British administration and the British army in
Egypt, or the clandestine negotiations with the Sharif of Mecca,
to which the Viceroy's Government in India took wholehearted
exception. Until very recently (only in 1968 did the Foreign and
India Office files on the subject become available for public
inspection), Lawrence was the chief witness. His account, told in
resonant language and in the first-person, left many gaps. The
pressures brought to bear on McMahon and, through him, on the
Government at home in the white heat of the Dardanelles and
Mesopotamian disasters, are hinted at, but his story leaves many

questions unasked and unanswered; not least, the question why a wily old religious official of the Ottoman Empire, trained in Constantinople and known far and wide as a conspiratorial man, one of whose sons was vice-president of the Turkish Parliament and another the member for Jiddah, should be deemed a trustworthy ally by the 'intrusives'. If ambition and greed led him to betray his friends and masters in Constantinople, would the same qualities not make him a dubious colleague in war? And would not an alliance with the Sharif turn the other great men of Arabia, who enjoyed the loyalty of the desert tribes, against his new paymasters?

The details of the negotiations with the Sharif of Mecca which flowed from Kitchener's message to his son Abdullah in September 1914, have been set out in books and Parliamentary papers, in academic studies and in the correspondence columns of the press of many countries over a period of more than sixty years. They need no repetition here, except in so far as they concerned Wallier Parker.

Izzat Pasha, the Pan-Islamite included in the Parker–Lawrence notes, had taken up a voluntary exile in France after the accession of the Young Turks, but he retained a base in Damascus and was in touch with the Turkish leaders and with the Sharif. He contacted the British Foreign Office in December 1915 and met Sir Henry McMahon when the latter was on his way to Cairo in the same month, to offer his services as an intermediary with the Sharif. The FO and McMahon agreed that he was 'too dangerous'. The messenger chosen to take Kitchener's first communication to Mecca was the Egyptian Ali Effendi, father-in-law of Storrs's Persian secretary Ruhi. Ali was familiar with Abdullah, a frequent visitor to the family estates in Egypt, to whom the message was addressed: 'Tell Storrs to send a secret and carefully chosen messenger from me to the Sharif Abdullah . . .'.[1]

In July 1915, a shaikh of the Harb tribe, Muhammad ibn Arif Araifan, codenamed 'O', had taken over. And in October, Muhammad al Faruqi the Gallipoli deserter was on the scene, scurrying between Cairo and Mecca aboard HMS *Hardinge*, rowed ashore in *sambuqs* and dhows whose owners had been on the payrolls of Parker and Father Jaussen from the beginning of 1915.

By the end of 1915 the die was cast.

In return for his leadership of a rebellion against the Turks, Husain ibn Ali the Sharif of Mecca had been promised hegemony over all the lands of the Arabian peninsula, excepting Britain's pensioner states in the Gulf, Aden and the 'districts of Mersina and Alexandretta and portions of Syria lying to the west of the districts of Damascus, Hama, Homs, and Aleppo'. The Sharif had agreed to forgo the Basra vilayet (administrative region) temporarily, and the other 'special' British shaikhdoms, and Mersina and Alexandretta; but he did not renounce the last-named 'portions of Syria'. The wording of Britain's note excluding them was, in any case, imprecise.

McMahon had been advised and pressured by the 'Sharifites' of the intelligence office in Cairo. By the time a new GOC arrived in January 1916, when the Chief of the Imperial General Staff Sir Archibald Murray was appointed to dual control with Maxwell, it only remained for the military detail of the rebellion to be plotted. But by then the Dardanelles evacuation had been accomplished successfully and the chief military purpose of the Arab Revolt, a disturbance which might draw off the Turkish army reserves being thrown into that remorseless battle zone, was removed.

Lawrence set out the cast. 'We were not many; and nearly all of us rallied round Clayton, the chief of Intelligence, civil and military.' He was, said Lawrence, 'the perfect leader'. But Clayton had responsibilities to the Chief of Staff, General Sir Lynden Bell, and through him to the GOC. Another was the real leader. 'The first of us was Ronald Storrs, Oriental Secretary of the Residency, the most brilliant Englishman in the Near East, and subtly efficient, despite his diversion of energy in love of music and letters, of sculpture, painting, of whatever was beautiful in the world's fruit.' Of the others, there was George Lloyd, 'We would not have done so much so soon without his partnership'; Mark Sykes, in effect the liaison between War Office and Foreign Office Intelligence in Whitehall, 'a bundle of prejudices, intuitions, half-sciences'; Hogarth, 'our father confessor and adviser'; Cornwallis, 'a man rude to look upon'. Others brought up the rear: 'Newcombe, Parker, Herbert, Graves, all of the creed, and labouring stoutly after their fashion.'

In December 1915 Sir Mark Sykes, back in London after a visit to Clayton and Storrs in Cairo, proposed to the Government a Cairo Bureau which would be independent of the GOC, and would be the composite responsibility of War Office, Admiralty, Foreign Office and India Office.[2]

On 10 December the Secretary of State for India sent details of the plan to the Viceroy, telling him that Mark Sykes would be in charge of the Bureau, assisted by Philip Graves and Maj. Hennessy of the Indian Army. He received a short answer which said that the Indian Government had no confidence in the suggested staff. The Indian under-secretary Sir Arthur Hirtzel noted: 'Government of India distrust personnel and I am not surprised at their hesitation.' On 6 January Prime Minister Asquith ordered a meeting at the War Office to finalize plans for the Bureau on that day, to be attended by all the political and military intelligence chiefs. It was to have been called the 'Islamic Bureau', the name given by the German Foreign Office to its Eastern propaganda machine. The meeting decided that it should be called the 'Arab Bureau' and that its titular chief should be Mark Sykes, and its acting head Col. Parker, who was acceptable to the Government of India and to Whitehall and Cairo.

Wallier Parker had taken no part in the Sharifian negotiations. Neither had Newcombe. Both were professional soldiers who obeyed the instructions of the Chief of Staff, and kept a discreet distance between themselves and the self-appointed policy makers in their midst. None the less, they retained a surprising admiration for companions who were regarded with little affection by the staff officers in general.

There is no evidence from the records of the Arab Bureau that Parker ever took an active part in its affairs. From the outset, Hogarth was its leading light, directing its day-to-day activities as a unit of the second echelon of Cairo Intelligence. Parker and Newcombe, working for the first echelon with Col. Holdich, Murray's intelligence chief, continued to look after the espionage activities of their agents in Sinai and Syria respectively, and in the former's case continuing to probe the Hijaz coastal regions where most of the Arabs seemed still to be loyal to the Turks.

In June 1916, Storrs went down the Red Sea to Jiddah to finalize the arrangement with the Sharif and to witness the declaration of the revolt. That event had a most indeterminate history. It had been planned originally for July. Then for 16 June. Then for 10 June. When Storrs met the Sharif's youngest son Zaid on 6 June he was told that it had started the previous day, 5 June.

In July 1916 there was another Turco-German assault on Suez along the Arish road, led this time by Kress von Kressenstein. It was no more successful than before, and once again the German officer's careful preparation allowed his army to escape virtually unscathed. But Kitchener's protégés in Cairo had by then hatched their diversionary plot.

Hogarth, often the recrudescent undergraduate, composed a rhyme to commemorate the formation of the Arab Bureau and added some names to Lawrence's list in so doing. Symes (Secretary to the Sirdar of the Egyptian army, General Sir Reginald Wingate), Dawnay (Alan, brother of the man who would become Allenby's deputy Chief of Staff, General Guy Dawnay), Mackintosh, Fielding, Macindoe and Wordie, backroom boys at the Savoy Hotel who would retain their anonymity to the end.[3] Parker prepared to journey down the Red Sea to follow the desert war as the senior British intelligence officer in the Hijaz.

6
The Desert War

> Few people, even those who knew all the negotiations, had
> really believed that the Sharif would fight; consequently his
> eventual rebellion and opening of his coast to our ships and help
> took us and them by surprise.
>
> T. E. Lawrence, *Seven Pillars of Wisdom*

1916 was a year of mixed hope and despair, of reappraisal on all
sides. In January the Dardanelles evacuation was completed, and
the British force in Mesopotamia which had advanced almost to
the gates of Baghdad was driven back to a village at a bend of the
Tigris river known as Kut al Amara, where it was besieged by a
Turkish army under the direction of the Prussian Field Marshal
von der Goltz. The German general who had plotted the Turco-
German success in the Dardanelles, Liman von Sanders, offered
his resignation, unable to endure any longer the political interference of Berlin and Constantinople, and the hero of that
campaign, Col. Mustafa Kamal Bey, the 'Grey Wolf', was posted
to the Caucasus by Enver to ensure that military renown did not
become a political threat. In Cairo, Clayton was driven from the
General Staff by the new GOC, Gen. Murray, and replaced as
military intelligence chief by Col. Holdich. Clayton became the
effective head of the Arab Bureau,[1] the affairs of which were of no
concern to Murray. Lawrence was transferred from the General
Staff to the Bureau. In London, the Directorate of Military
Operations which had hitherto controlled intelligence, was split,
and the Directorate of Military Intelligence came into being, with

Gen. Macdonogh at its head. M12(b) became responsible for the
Ottoman Empire, Arabia and Persia. The Sharifian negotiations
reached a climax in February and Gertrude Bell departed from
Cairo for Delhi to sell the idea of the Arab Revolt to the Viceroy.
Meanwhile, the Sharif was making overtures to the Turks and
demanding money and arms from Britain. One of Britain's best-
informed Arab agents, Sayyid Mustafa, told Clayton that the
Sharif was 'inwardly pro-Turk'. His son Faisal was in Damascus
in March with Jamal Pasha and the young German staff officer
Maj. von Stotzingen who was preparing to lead a German mission
to Mecca. In the same month Lawrence boarded the SS *Royal
George*, bound for Basra where he would meet up with Aubery
Herbert from the Arab Bureau, and with an Arab nationalist
delegation led by Dr Cashar Rahman Shahbander of Damascus,
and Aziz al Masri, the Arab-Circassian officer of the Ottoman
army whom Kitchener had rescued from sentence of death in
Constantinople before the war. Lawrence and Herbert had secret
instructions to attempt to bribe the Turks to let the besieged force
at Kut al Amara off the hook. The generals in Mesopotamia
cold-shouldered the Englishmen and the Arabs who descended
from Cairo, however, and Lawrence never forgave them. 'Third
raters', he called them. Sir Percy Cox, the Chief Political Officer
in Mesopotamia, returned the compliment. He called Lawrence
'hopeless', and Hubert Young who would shortly join in the Hijaz
campaign, was 'shocked' by the conduct of the diminutive
Englishman in their midst. And during this time, Mark Sykes, the
founder of the Arab Bureau, was secretly negotiating with M.
Georges-Picot, the man who had betrayed the Arab nationalists
to Jamal, an agreement which would divide between Britain and
France the territories which McMahon, with Foreign Office
approval, had promised to the Sharif. In June, War Office secret
telegrams reported (on the 11th): 'Arab Bureau officers back. One
group believe that revolt genuine and inevitable, though preparations faulty through ignorance of modern warfare, and inclined to
leave too much to luck.'[2] And on the 12th: Senior Naval Officer,
Red Sea, to DNI, 'Arabs greatly exaggerate strength of opposing
forces.' On 14 June the Government of India received word that

HMS *Hardinge* and *Fox* had shelled Turkish positions north of Jiddah: 'Have informed Secretary of State of our grave concern . . . Viceroy and Indian Government totally opposed to Sharif's action.' Capt. Weldon, still the intelligence officer aboard HMS *Anne*, the famous old tramp *Aenne Rickmers*, received Clayton, Cornwallis and Ali Bey (a Sudanese officer in the Egyptian army who had been nominated the Sharif's Chief of Staff) at Suez. They brought with them £30,000 in gold for the Sharif, to be handed over to the agent 'O' at Port Sudan. That agent, Araifan, had already been followed by the Turkish secret police who had told the Sharif to arrest him. But by now the Turks had withdrawn from Mecca and Jiddah and so he could enter the Hijaz safely.[3] On 27 June, *Anne* took Col. C. E. Wilson, Wingate's man at Port Sudan, to Jiddah as the Sirdar's special representative to the Sharif and head of Britain's military mission.[4] But he was to be called 'Mr', as Cairo wished to hide from Indian Muslims the fact that Britain had a military mission in the Islamic holy land. On 14 June, the Secretary of State for India, Austen Chamberlain, stung by acid comments from Delhi, had told the Viceroy 'HMG and not the Cairo Bureau, will decide all questions of policy.' On 10 July, after several false reports, the Turkish garrison at Mecca surrendered to the Sharif's men. The Turks decided to concentrate at Madina, the Prophet's city, under Gen. Fakhri Pasha, and at Maan, the two key-points on the Hijaz railway. They were to hold out for the rest of the war, undisturbed by the Arab Revolt, in what was the truly remarkable achievement of a very questionable campaign. Soon after the declaration of the rebellion, McMahon transmitted to London the Sharif's request for an allowance of £125,000 a month. The request was granted despite Treasury opposition. The India Office recorded: 'Arabs are somewhat difficult allies.'

Parker had spent the early part of 1916 in Cairo, interrogating Turkish prisoners of war and conducting reconnaissance along the Red Sea coast from Ismailiya where he was in charge of the Intelligence office from January to March. Early in August it was decided that he should go to the Hijaz as liaison intelligence officer, working with Wilson at Jiddah but reporting – by that strange arrangement which reflected the rivalries of Cairo – to the Sirdar, the Arab Bureau and its new chief Clayton, and to the General Staff (I) in Ismailiya under Holdich.

14 August. Left Cairo 7 a.m. General Dobell [Murray's commander Eastern Force], Russell [staff officer] and St Quentin [Lt. Doynel de St Q, French Staff Officer attached British GHQ] also passengers. (To GHQ Ismailiya.) Spoke to A. Dawnay. Lunched with Jennings Bramly. Met Cairo train and Maj. Mackenzie with letter for Wilson [Jiddah] and £300 gold for me. Took 2.5 train to Suez. With me Shaikh Muhammad Bey Suleiman and two Arabs and Shaikh Rafia al Dhaba and two Arabs. No reply from Boyle [SNO] to repeated messages.
  Sailed in HMS *Dufferin* 5.30 p.m.

15/16 August. Southing.

17 August.Jiddah at 8.45 a.m. Turkish prisoners, soldiers, civilians and families embark. Ashore at 11.20 steamboat and whaler. Walked to consulate and missed Wilson on way. He taking launch to *Dufferin*. Followed and later went [together] to see Captain Boyle on *Fox*. Left Jiddah 3 p.m.

19 August. Suez.

GHQ(I) 19 August 1916: Telegram
I have so far been unable to carry out the work desired in the neighbourhood of Al Wejh and Dhiba. On the 14th Lt.-Col. O'Sullivan informed me that no reply had been received from the SNO making a ship available to proceed to these places. . . . The first opportunity will be about 25th August when Capt. Boyle has promised HMS*Scotia*. . . . I had the opportunity at Jiddah of seeing both Capt. Boyle and Col. Wilson and speaking of the project of the destruction of the Railway. Col. Wilson is pressing the Sharif to encompass the destruction of the coast garrisons north of Wejh, and with the same object has written to the Sharif Faisal asking the latter to meet him at Yanbo, when he intends to ask him for the men necessary for the task, offering to Faisal to convey them up the coast in one of HM ships.

I suggest that one field-gun or light howitzer, if available with such a force, is likely to shorten the time necessary to enforce a surrender very considerably, especially since the garrison are probably in the heavily walled forts which exist along the coast, and which, in the case of Wejh, lies about 4 miles inland, invisible from the sea, and probably unassailable by ship's guns. The actual number of the garrisons is uncertain. One report places the numbers at 2,000 between Al Wejh and Aqaba (including these places). Another report gives: Al Wejh 300 men under Naji Bey, Dhiba 500 men, Khuraiba 200 men.

Another report, the latest apparently, gave 200 men with two mountain guns at the inland port of al Wejh. Whatever the number , and Col. Wilson appears to think all these reports much exaggerated, there is little doubt that the Turks are anxious about the railway line, that they have enforced the coast garrisons, and that they have regular and very frequent messengers both from Dhiba to Tabuk and from al Wejh to al Ala. Col. Wilson's view of a landing at Aqaba was that if a withdrawal were made without any good result having been effected, it would involve a loss of prestige. As regards a raid on the railway he was inclined to think that it was hardly worth while trying unless some serious more or less permanent damage could be done, such as the blowing in of the tunnel. He suggested that in case any operations were undertaken the Sharif should be requested to supply an agent to assist the Intelligence or Political Officer with the force. Col. Wilson enquired whether twenty of the Amir Faisal's men could be trained at Suez in the use of explosives as best employed against a railway line. I informed him that I was sure it could be arranged. Finally, it is not possible for me to make any definite suggestions as to the Railway until further information is available, and I am preparing to embark again on HMS *Scotia* with a view to endeavouring to obtain it. ACP.

Parker was unable to leave for Wejh during August as HMS *Scotia* was not available. He left Suez again on 3 September aboard HMS *Fox*, a seaplane carrier, and arrived at Kadima at 9 a.m. on 6 September. The day before he left Suez, a conference took place at Ismailiya between Gen. Murray and the High Commissioner Sir Henry McMahon, at which Wilson gave evidence on the military situation in the Hijaz, and McMahon described the initiation of the discussions with the Sharif as 'the worst day of my life'. With regard to a proposed landing at Aqaba, Wilson told the meeting that the Sharif would allow no landings by troops on the Hijaz coast. Wilson was at Kadima waiting for Parker by the 6th.

6 September. Kadima 9 a.m. *Dufferin* with Wilson there. Also the *Arethusa*. Transferred to *Dufferin*. *Arethusa* left with rifles for Jiddah. Areifan came on board with letters written by Husain of Rabegh to say that he was collecting tribes and was to arrive at Kadima morning of 8th. Protested loyalty to Sharif. Wilson had interviewed Zaid in morning. *Anne* arrived before sunset. Letters sent to Zaid [younger son of Sharif Husain, at this time eighteen years of age].

7 September. Flight by one aeroplane 5.30–6.30 a.m. Araifan came on board at 10 p.m. to say the Husain of Rabegh was surely coming on 8th. Brought letter from Zaid asking for ships to wait and then go on to Rabegh perhaps on Saturday. If not . . . one [ship] and a seaplane. Reply sent by Wilson that as soon as Husain has sworn fealty he must go. Cannot wait and cannot keep one ship. Ruhi [Storrs's Secretary] went ashore with Araifan to bring news as to results of meeting.

*8 September.*Ruhi and Araifan came aboard with letter from Zaid at 2 p.m. Husain of Rabegh had arrived with following of many men early and . . . somewhat frightened. He protested that he had been loyal throughout. That he had sent on all rifles and ammunition to Ali and had receipts . . . Zaid replied that apart from giving proof or going into the past, what was his attitude now? Was he with the Turks of the Sharif, and if the latter would he swear an oath as dictated by him? The oath of allegiance was sworn. Ruhi entirely satisfied that everything completed in good faith and impressed with the strong character of Husain. Letter sent to Zaid warning him to keep a watch on Husain. Ship left 3.30 p.m. for Yanbo.

9 September. Yanbo 9 a.m. Meeting with Faisal.

*10 September.*Yanbo. HMS *Fox* arrived but did not enter harbour. *Anne* remained at Sharm Yanbo where she grounded. Capt. Boyle came on *Hardinge* for meeting with Faisal. Also present three Juhaina shaikhs, Saad Ghoneim, Sharif Jabir. *Dufferin* left 1 p.m. for Suez with Col. Wilson. Grain for Um Lejj and 100-odd Arabs shipped on *Hardinge*. Left at 4 p.m. Reports on Wejh etc. Suleiman Pasha and sons said to be held prisoner by Turks as hostages for tribe. Force of 195 Turks said to be on way from Muwailah to Um Lejj in three *sambuqs* and last reported at Masra al Arjaj some seven miles south of Wejh. Another report of doubtful authenticity that 8,000 Turks and Arabs are on way from Tabuk to the coast – object unknown. *Hardinge* put down Boyle at Sharm Yanbo. *Fox* in Sharm Yanbo north of *Anne* which appeared to be on reef and not much chance of getting off on account of strong north wind. Proceeding at slow speed through night [aboard *Hardinge*].

Parker contacted Ismailiya from the *Hardinge*, with details of the complex comings and goings at Yanbo and Kadima.

To GHQ (I), 10 September 1916: Telegram
[After recounting the events of the past four days, including the flight of seaplanes over Kadima on the morning of the 8th which 'greatly impressed the assembled Arabs', and the departure of Zaid with Shaikh Husain and a following of some thousands for Rabegh, he reported the meeting with Faisal:]

During the morning of the 9th the Sharif Faisal came on board the *Dufferin* and had a long conversation with Col. Wilson, at which I was present. Wilson explained exactly what had happened at Kadima with reference to Shaikh Husain Mubarak of Rabegh[5] [Husain Mabeirig of Lawrence's version, who eventually deserted the Sharif and took to the hills having decided that the Turks were likely to be victorious].

Faisal was not entirely reassured as to Husain's attitude and expressed fears that he might still find opportunities to go over to the Turks. Throughout his conversation the one point he was apprehensive of was Rabegh, and the continued presence of Shaikh Husain there, even though under the observation of Sharif Zaid and others, was obviously disquieting to him. The situation described by Faisal was as follows:

Faisal's force [4,000 men armed with British rifles, no artillery] now confronts the main Turkish advance south at a place not far from Bir

Abbas on the road from Madina to Rabegh [Darb Sultani], the Turkish force consisting of twelve battalions, or about 12,000 men, with 16 mountain guns and 2 guns of heavier calibre. The country there is mountainous. Faisal expected a determined attempt to break through on the part of the Turks within a period of three or four days. He did not anticipate that he would be able to hold there if they did so, and he greatly feared the effects of a defeat on the Arabs with him, many of whom might desert. Ali's force of 8,000 men [with British rifles], 2 captured Turkish guns and 2 maxims, is said to be not far east of Bir al Mashi and is there facing a not considerable body of Turks who are apparently only keeping him in play and not endeavouring to advance South. Ali, though not actually on the Eastern pilgrim route from Madina to Mecca, is watching it and ready to attack any force moving by it. What Turkish forces are actually facing Ali is not clear, but they are probably not large since he appears to have liberty of movement.

Intercommunication between Ali and Faisal, as one might expect, appears to be most indifferent. Some fighting is said to be going on within ten kilometres of Madina itself, which is reported to be almost bare of troops. Raids on the Turkish lines of communication are said to have been carried out recently and small convoys cut up, the Arabs capturing 100 camels on one occasion. The number of camels with the Turks is unknown, but they are said to be mostly supplied by Ibn Rashid. . . . A party of Arabs from Jauf is said to have arrived at Ali's camp. To the Juhaina, whose Shaikh, Saad Ghonaim, came in on Col. Wilson's last visit to Yanbo, Faisal had recently issued 3,500 rifles and instructions to take action against the railway in the neighbourhood of Bir Nasif. An additional 500 rifles he had given them to guard against any possible action by the Billi. Faisal had received satisfactory messages from the brother and son of Suleiman Pasha Abu Rifada [Chief of the Billi], the latter being expected almost immediately from Tabuk. Faisal hoped that the Billi would follow the Juhaina, and the Howaitat the Billi. Faisal estimates Turkish forces in and near Madina at 29 battalions or about 25,000 men, and he expressed the opinion that they would find it extremely difficult to send further reinforcements. Should the Arabs destroy the Madina forces, they could, Faisal thought, advance straight through Syria to Aleppo. Faisal explained the plan of operations which he favoured: His force should allow the Turks to pass through southwards, then cutting their lengthened line of communications and attacking them from the North while Ali, moving swiftly South, was to attack from the East, and the Rabegh force to hold them or attack them from the South.

The above is the gist of Faisal's talk. The salient points were his inability to stop a determined advance by the Turks, his fears of the effects on his Arabs of a serious defeat, and his apprehensions of treachery by Husain of Rabegh. He continually begged for a few British troops at Rabegh as a visible sign of British support, to reassure and give confidence to the Arabs. In the absence of a great deal of necessary information, topographical and otherwise, which is not available, it is difficult to appreciate clearly the situation. But there is no reason to doubt the information given by Faisal except that the Turkish numbers may be somewhat exaggerated.

Parker concluded his lengthy report on the situation at 10 September with a plea to GHQ to send a token force to Rabegh, at least until the fall of Taif (the summer resort of Mecca in the Hijaz mountains to which most of the Turkish garrison had repaired in May, and which had been under siege since 9 June by a force of 5,000 Arabs under Abdullah, the Sharif's second son). He argued that the Sharif had agreed to accept Christian help (a matter about which the Sharif in fact changed his mind almost hourly), and that the withdrawal of such a force after it had achieved its limited objective, would be proof of Britain's sincerity in not coveting the Islamic holy places. He also warned that the Turks were preparing a 'Mahmal',[6] a ceremonial litter, to take from Madina to Mecca, with the Sharif Ali Haider, the pretender to the Sharifate of Mecca.[7]

Parker's telegram concluded: 'To obtain better information on the positions and numbers of the forces is most essential. This can best be done by aeroplanes working from Yanbo or from an advanced base east of Yanbo.'

11 September. Hardinge reached Hassani Island [off Um Lejj] and anchored 7 a.m. Steamboat towing rowing boat to Um Lejj with Ruhi and Saad Ghoneim. Orders for eight *sambuqs* immediately to put out to ship to land cargo. Steamboat to wait until Ruhi and Saad Ghoneim have collected all possible information and then return with them. Juhaina Arabs aboard *Hardinge* much interested in gold teeth. . . . Ruhi and Arabs return at 4 p.m. Brought Sharif Ghalib, brother of Sharif Muhammad Ali, on board as Faisal had ordered him to report himself to Yanbo. Report of 195 Turks in three *sambuqs* on way to Um Lejj. Expected to arrive tonight.

News of Suleiman Pasha Abu Rifada is that he was to leave Al Ala today for Al Wejh. He is said to be surely for the Sharif in spite of having accepted 300 camel loads of stores recently from the Turks. Faisal's messenger left to meet him on road and is to be at Wejh on Wednesday with Abu Rifada or with news of him. No news of garrisons farther north. *Anne* to be off Marduna Island and plane to fly to Hassani [island] tomorrow morning.

12 September. Fox and *Anne* arrived early. Aeroplanes up at 7 a.m. and reconnoitred Um Lejj. Another went off at 8.30 to reconnoitre coast.

Ruhi sent ashore at 8.30 to arrange for Saad Ghoneim to organize defences against attack by Turks. Also to send two or three men along coast to get news of Turks and the three dhows [previously *sambuqs*, smaller craft]. Ruhi and Saad returned 4 p.m. Saad's father appointed to take command at Um Lejj. *Fox, Hardinge* and *Anne* left for Wejh 5 p.m. Suleiman abu Rifada due at Wadi Miyah today.

13 September. At Al Wejh by daybreak. *Fox* had a man overboard and so slightly delayed. Ruhi went into harbour in steamboat under white flag. Man came to beach and Ruhi gave him letter to Commandant – surrender or accept consequences. No reply. . . . Ships opened fire on trenches marked by seaplanes. When approaching Wejh groups of men seen going NE, presumably to line trenches. Thirty seen on skyline at one time. *Anne* at anchor near Sharm Habban. *Hardinge* left 9.15 a.m. and anchored off Al Miyah. Shaikhs Jabir and Saad Ghoneim with two Arabs landed; to try to get news. 2 p.m. steamboat sent in for Arab who came down on camel and was waving. Proved to be one of Faisal's messengers to Suleiman abu Rifada. They had arrived at Fahaiman's house [Billi shaikh] very early on 13th. One of then left with Fahaiman for Suleiman's house 1½ days distant. Other had come straight to coast at Wadi al Miyah. Fahaiman of opinion that Suleiman was for the Sharif but messenger could not guarantee that he [Suleiman] would come to ship. Turks at Wejh said to have sheep ready to slay in honour of Suleiman's arrival. Messenger given £5 and landed again with instructions to ride as quickly as possible to Suleiman Pasha and ask him to come Wadi al Miyah. Messenger estimated that Pasha could not be there before midday Saturday [16th]. 5.10 p.m. proceeded south to Arja to look for and destroy dhows and so prevent Turks moving. Seaplanes flew along coast, but light going. Camels seen in thorn scrub. No dhows.

14 September. Hardinge to Minaibara to look for Turks. Saad Ghoneim allowed to land with 25 Sharifian Arabs at 9.15 a.m. and walked south finding boy who showed them Turkish stores. Advancing south Arabs engaged by Turkish force which was shelled by ship. Some Arabs returned to ship with one wounded asking for more ammunition and help. Ammunition given and 15 men landed. Ship's fire directed by shore party, probably caused some casualties. Dhows destroyed by gunfire. Party of Turks attempted to outflank Arabs but destroyed by ship's fire. Lieut. Allen wounded. Landing party and Arabs withdrawn to ship without further casualties. Turks said to be the party of 195 [11 Sept] but this is unlikely, and actual number not more than 40. [Weldon records, in *Hard Lying*, 14 September. Seaplanes reconnoitre over Wejh. Weldon at Rabegh with Parker entertaining Aziz al Masri who had arrived to take command of Sharifian forces.]

15 September. Off Al Wejh. No movement near town. To *Daedalus* at night for man who had died preceding day.

16 September. At anchor 7.30 a.m., Al Miyah. Two men seen on shore; one proved to be Itamid al Gedaia (messenger) instructed to proceed to Abu Rifada with letters on Wednesday. Reached Suleiman's home at wells of Al Khautla [wadi joining W. Hamdth] Friday forenoon. Three hundred Arabs with him [Suleiman]. Latter gave messenger letter saying he would be at Wadi al Miyah 1 p.m. on 16 September. Messenger met Arab who said Turks from Al Arja were retiring inland and were in difficulties for want of water. One man killed and one wounded [among Arab force], estimated they had inflicted six casualties.

1 p.m. messenger arrived to say that Suleiman Pasha was on his way.
Shaikhs and Ruhi ashore. Cavalcade of fifty men on camels appeared
going down wadi at 2.30. Proceeding very slowly they made their way to
north side of valley where they disappeared from view. Later shaikhs
appeared and met with our group. I went ashore and spoke with
Suleiman Pasha. A sly-looking man with beard dyed black. Interview
most unsatisfactory. Ended at 5.40.

To the Amir Faisal Bey
[After compliments.] I regret to inform you that the attitude of Suleiman
Pasha abu Rifada is most uncompromising. The Sharif Jabir Shaikh
Muhammad Jubara will no doubt inform you of all that passed.
Suleiman Pasha stated first that many of his Arabs were in the pay of the
Turks and that it was impossible to do more than try gradually to obtain
their adherence to the Sharif. Any precipitate action could he felt
throw the Billi in with the Turks. Asked how long it might take him to
get all his Arabs together for the Sharif, he gave six months as the
shortest time.

It was pointed out to him that by this time the war would probably be
over and now was the time for action to help the Sharif to a speedy
victory.

All arguments were to no avail and I finally told him that most people
might think he was waiting to see the result of the war before showing
himself actively for the Sharif since, according to general report, no
person was said to have more power over his tribesmen than he. He
replied that if such things were said it were better to say at once that he
was allied to the Turks. It was then pointed out to him that the business
in hand concened you and your father the Sharif, and the English only as
assisting you, and it was therefore suggested that he should appoint a
brother or son to proceed to you in order to keep you informed of all
that occurred. He refused to promise to send any relative but said he
would send letters. He said he required no money or arms and that if he
asked for money it would be after doing what he could and not before.
He suggested towards the end that trade might be reopened with Suez
from his ports, to which I made no reply. It is obvious that as matters
stand this should not be considered. And thus ended the interview. Most
unsatisfactorily, but I feel convinced that had the conversation continued

for a week we should have advanced no further.

ACP 16.9.16. Off Wejh

On the day of Parker's interview with Abu Rifada, 'M', Britain's Chief of Intelligence at Berne, European HQ of the secret service, reported to the DMI in London that 9,000 Turkish regulars had left Damascus for Madina under Jamal's ex-Chief of Staff Fuad Pasha (a Francophile officer who had been military attaché in Paris). Three days earlier Gen. Murray had again met the High Commissioner McMahon in Cairo to discuss help for the Sharif. On the 16th, too, Lawrence, still observing events in the desert war from the Savoy Hotel in Cairo, had another conversation with his French friend Lieut. St Quentin, in the course of which he talked of the possibility of blowing up the track of the Hijaz railway.[8] On 19 September, Berne – reported[9] that a Turkish emissary had arrived in Riyadh to meet Ibn Saud, and that the Sharif had sent gifts of £10,000 each (from British funds) to the pro-Turk leader Ibn Rashid at Hail and to Ibn Saud.

At 6.30 a.m. on Monday 18 September Parker arrived back at Suez aboard HMS *Fox* with a report on the Sharif's campaign for GHQ (I), bearing that day's date. It recapitulated much of the information contained in his diary since his last report dated 10 September. But there were some important additions and asides.

The objects of the visit to Al Wejh remain entirely unsatisfied. No projects of raids on the Hijaz railway through the Billi country can be considered with matters as they stand. Suleiman Pasha Abu Rifada, fresh from a visit to Jamal Pasha, and no doubt with his pockets recently filled with gold, is definitely pro-Turk for the moment, though he states that his sympathies are with the Sharif. He is unimpressed by our naval demonstrations, since they lead to nothing, while he appears to rate very highly the Turkish military strength and the numbers of Arabs assisting them. Possibly, so long as Abu Rifada continues to state himself to be sympathetic to the Sharifian cause, the latter may prefer leaving matters as they stand, rather than naming him publicly as an enemy. It is a weak policy which has little to recommend it, but it is difficult to see how else the Sharif can act unless given assistance. The temporary occupation of

Wejh, by a British force if necessary, and a subsequent ultimatum by the Sharif to Abu Rifada, followed by Juhaina raids from the south, is the most desirable action and should have an excellent effect on the Arabs everywhere, as well as a correspondingly depressing effect on the Turks.

He also gave his blessing to the idea of sending a force to Aqaba, an operation which would in the view of most officers at GHQ be accomplished easily by a naval landing party, though the feat would eventually be achieved a year later from inland.[10] Indeed, in February 1915, after the Suez attack had been repulsed, a French naval party from the *Desaix* had landed at Aqaba and its Turkish garrison took to its heels.[11]

Action taken at Al Wejh as suggested above, in no way weakens the arguments for an occupation of Aqaba, and the failure to obtain Arab sympathy and help at Wejh makes the latter operation all the more essential in order to obtain a base from which to approach the Arabs, obtain information, and possibly plan raids . . . in each case, however, the occupation (except for Aqaba) is only to tide us over a crisis in Sharifian affairs.

Five days later he was on his way down the Red Sea again, this time aboard the flag ship of the C-in-C, Admiral Sir Rosslyn Wemyss. His party was preceded on the voyage to Jiddah by a French military mission, led by Col. Brémond, which had been conferring with the GOC in Cairo earlier in the month. On 20 September the CIGS, Sir William Robertson, had sent Murray a telegram:[12] 'Decided to send aeroplanes to help Sharif.' A week later he was to instruct the GOC:[13] 'Do not send troops to Rabegh.' By now, Wingate had virtually taken over all dealing with the Sharif on Britain's side, and Parker was instructed to send all reports to *Arbur*, the telegraphic address of the Arab Bureau, as well as to GHQ.

23 Sept. Saturday. Embarked on HMS *Euryalus* at 7.30 a.m. with Maj. Bannatyne, Lieut. Brigstocke RAMC, Lieut. Perry RE. Instructions to proceed to Jiddah there to ascertain from Wilson where aeroplanes are to be landed and then to proceed with party to examine and report by wireless. My personal responsibility to be political, i.e. safety of RFC flights on shore without escort [the Sharif it seems had agreed to Christian pilots operating from land bases but not troops].[14] Examination of locality should include consideration of landing a battalion as escort, or a brigade. Admiral suggested a conference on arrival at Jiddah and mentioned possibility of using Hassani as aeroplane base. Dine with Admiral.

24 September. Southing. Wireless received – fall of Taif. 1,800 Turks taken prisoner [the Turkish garrison had finally surrendered on the 22nd after heroic resistance to a vastly superior Arab force while under siege for nearly four months, and intermittent bombardment by Egyptian artillery]. Admiral is asking Capt. Boyle to come on board and bring Col. Wilson on arrival at Jiddah.

25 September. Southing.

26 September. Arrive Jiddah 3.30 p.m. HMS *Fox* and *Hardinge* at anchor. Also French yacht *Hadj* and two pilgrim ships [the French delegation had arrived just before them, and remarkably the annual pilgrimage – the Hajj – to Mecca had taken place in September with faithful from as far afield as Indonesia, India, and Egypt, and even Turkey, in attendance]. Boyle and Wilson came aboard. Wilson wants flight at Rabegh to watch for advance of Turks. Arabs are entrenching under Ali and Nuri [Nuri Said, the Baghdadi staff officer of the Turkish army who had been captured by the British in Mesopotamia, now second in command to Aziz al Masri, Enver's old rival in the Turkish army, who in September was appointed chief of the Sharif's army]. Husain of Rabegh said to have fled to the hills on news of Ali's approach with 1,000 men. Turks said to have retired to Bir Darwish on account of scarcity of water. Boyle to keep a ship permanently at Rabegh.

27 September. 9 a.m. Ahmad Pasha, Amir al Hajj (chief of the pilgrim caravan) came aboard from *Hardinge* dressed in bath towel secured by Sam Browne belt. 9.30 a.m. Admiral, Capt. Burmester (RN), Storrs, Flag-Lieutenant (Cdr. Neville), and self to shore. [Storrs, ever fastidious

of the company he kept had remained in seclusion aboard the *Euryalus*.]
Met by Sharif Muhsin and guard of honour. Coffee. To Sharif Muhsin's
(office), more coffee. Ride to French consulate to call on Col. Brémond.
Ride to British consulate. Ride to HQ municipality, more coffee. Return
to ship 1 p.m. Sharif Muhsin called in afternoon.

28 September. Admiral and officers ashore to see pilgrim carpet [from
Egypt] landed. *Hardinge* sailed at 9 a.m. (with Admiral's party).
Reached Rabegh before sunset. Message sent ashore asking for horses
for Admiral and party to ride. Verbal message brought by interpreter
Ruhi (on *Dufferin*) that British officers could not land without order
from Sharif. Ruhi presented order to Sharif who was alone at the time.
He shook his head and remarked that it was a difficult matter. Later he
called Zaid and Nuri and spoke with them in Turkish. Ruhi sent ashore
with very stiff letter from Wilson. Wire at same time to Sharif reporting
matter and requesting necessary instructions. Ruhi returned at midnight
saying it was all a misunderstanding. Wire to Sharif cancelled.

29 September. Sharif Ali came on board at 8 a.m. accompanied by Nuri.
Later entire party ashore, mounting at 9 a.m. Round right flank, past
fort and down N side of wadi. Returned to shore at 12. Sites for
aerodrome. *Hardinge* left for Jiddah 4.30 p.m.

Telegram to ARBUR
Situation at Rabegh is that about 5,000 Arabs under Sharif Ali are
entrenching a position about 4 miles from shore. The left flank can be
covered by ships' fire at about 6,000 yards. Husain of Rabegh said to be
in the hills with following of perhaps 500 but is said to be going to
Mecca. No sign of Turkish advance at present. There is a report of two
aeroplanes at Madina. Abdullah with 4,000 men said to be advancing on
Eastern road. Ali asks urgently for 3 Q.F. mountain batteries for which
he has personnel. On receipt of these Rabegh force will probably move
north to attack Turks. SNO keeping a ship here at present and if planes
landed guarantees continued presence. He would reinforce with a
second ship if Turkish attack imminent. Feasibility of advanced aeroplane
base doubtful since careful advanced reconnaissance is essential and
may be impracticable. I do not recommend flight being landed without

escort. Aerodrome site not yet fixed but almost certainly would require protection. Arab escort could probably not be spared from main position besides being unsatisfactory for obvious reasons. Also efficiency of flight personnel much reduced if carrying out guard and other camp duties. I consider that escort should not be less than a battalion. Utility of [land-based] aeroplanes seems to me to depend on feasibility of advanced base, and if work along Sultani road only required and if maps are anyway accurate seaplanes working up to Buraika can do it as well unless Turkish aeroplanes appear.

To sum up:

Turkish advance south is problematical. Arabs intend to advance north if they get the batteries asked for. Seaplanes can reconnoitre Sultani road as efficiently as aeroplanes if latter without advanced base. Escort of one battalion necessary if planes landed.

Recommendations:

Earliest possible despatch of mountain artillery. Cancellation of order for aeroplanes if above are sent. A Political Officer to remain here, namely myself, to keep Wilson informed until Arabs move. This Wilson wishes. My party will continue reconnaissance and I propose to send them north first opportunity, after completion remaining here myself.

Parker 29.9.16.

30 September. Examined site for aeroplanes in morning. Excellent site close to Custom House approved by Bannatyne. Alternative site in case first becomes muddy in winter about 1,500 yards off. Wire sent accordingly to Wilson. Arrangements for sketching party, Bray [Maj. N. N. E. Bray, arrived as staff officer (I) to Wilson on 10th, after briefing at WO, London], Perry, Galbraith (RNVR) to make sketch following day, assisted by cartographic officer. Another party consisting of self, Bannatyne, Brigstocke to examine possible route for motor tenders to get north of Rabegh on to plain, for possibilities of using cars to supply advanced landing ground up Sultani road, also bearing in mind [use of] armed motor cars in defence of position.

Parker to Wilson, 30 September (wireless)
Site for aerodrome fifty yards from sea examined and found excellent by Bannatyne. Report that Turks advancing south but value of report uncertain.

Letter to the Amir Ali Bey, 30 September

I have received Nuri Bey's letter and I regret that you are unable to come to see me today since this causes delay. And before any assistance can be supplied by HMG it is essential that full and detailed information must be obtained of the locality and conditions, and it is necessary therefore to make a map and to examine water supply. Special officers have been sent for this purpose and have only a limited number of days before they return to Egypt. Today has been wasted. Will you please inform me whether you still wish aeroplanes to be sent here. I am telegraphing to Wilson Pasha informing of the delay in my work and have requested him to tell your father the Sharif. I trust that you will be able to make all arrangements for my officers to work tomorrow after our meeting.

1 October. Rabegh. Both parties on beach at 6 a.m. Nuri arrived 6.15 with animals and begged that neither party approach palm trees nearer than 500 yards, as there were irresponsible Arabs who might fire from among date groves and that the previous night a man had been shot through the thigh. Pointed out to Nuri that . . . it was his job to detail such escorts as might be necessary to ensure safety. This he could surely do with 500 men at his disposal. Nuri regretted that he could not ensure safety unless party kept away from palms. He suggested parties should occupy themselves on beach and up to 500 yards from groves [the silly argument is recounted in detail but is omitted here. The Sharif Ali was asked to attend and adjudicate, but he could not spare the time, and the officers eventually returned to the ship rather than be used for target practice.]

Sudanese boy, deserter from Husain Mubarak (of Rabegh) took refuge on ship. He was sure that Husain intended joining Turks in Madina. Now he gave out that he was going to Mecca (after a meeting with the Sharif Zaid; his harem had already been despatched to Madina), though only deterred from attacking Rabegh by presence of ships and seaplanes. He had armed 300 of Baladiya tribe but they would not face seaplanes. Arms consist of ten loads (stolen) of British rifles with ammunition. Husain's five brothers with him but the Baladiya and their Shaikh, Muhammad, had all taken to their houses in Rabegh. Husain 6–8 hours away in hills. Men take him supplies by night.

Anne left with Bannatyne to reconnoitre possible bases further south.

As Parker and his companions waited at Rabegh for a guarantee of protection – they were, of course, unarmed – the Foreign Office in London logged copies of telegrams passing between Jiddah and Military Intelligence. Wilson sent a message to the Sharif on 1 October: 'Col. Parker and other officers sent to arrange for defence of Rabegh. Must be allowed to land.' Ruhi was at the Sharif's palace and he replied to Wilson by telephone at 9.30 p.m.: 'His Highness has gone to bed and I told the Secretary not to send message [to Ali in Rabegh] until H.H. adds to it – British officers and men allowed to land.' Wilson by WT to Cairo: 'Parker's men being sniped at by irresponsible Arabs.' Sharif to Ali Bey, 2 October: 'Agree to permit landings.'[15]

2 October. Ali Bey and Nuri arrived on board 8 a.m. Former expressed himself as desirous of assisting in every possible way but that there were . . . persons who might do things which he, Ali, would infinitely regret. No doubt of Ali's sincerity. I informed him that if he thought this he should detail escorts as would give rise to no risks of any kind. He had no objection to an escort of British troops being landed with aeroplanes. More, he would willingly see a large British force at Rabegh. Arrangements made for survey parties to land in afternoon. Arrangements made with Nuri for continuation of work next morning, wells to be examined and samples of water taken.

To Wilson Jiddah. Please repeat to Arbur
Hope to complete reconnaissance tomorrow and will summarize results by wire. Appreciation of military situation:

(1) Arab cause is successful if Mecca is denied to Turks.

(2) It is probable that lack of troops does not permit Turks to send more than one division south from Madina.

(3) According to all report such a force must move by Rabegh and therefore if Rabegh is held Arab cause is won.

(4) Opposition offered to a Turkish advance before arrival at Rabegh would be considerable but of a guerrilla nature.

(5) A Turkish division if successful in pressing through would probably succeed in capture of Rabegh from present garrison.

(6) From a political point of view the presence of a force of

two battalions British troops entrenched at Rabegh would probably deter Turks from undertaking an advance.

(7) From a military point of view a British Brigade landed two days before Turkish attack should surely beat off Turks.

As regards aeroplanes, they would not materially assist Arab resistance, though a valuable adjunct to a British force. Moreover, the landing of a flight of aircraft commits us to participate in land operations of which we cannot assure the success without landing troops. Also without advanced landing they are only slightly more efficient than seaplanes in the circumstances. Parker. 2.10.16

3 October. Sharif Abdullah has not left Taif and does not expect to move for another ten days. Faisal still at Bedur near Khaif. Perquistion made of Shaikh Husain's goods. Some supplies, rice and flour, supplied by British found. Also rifles. Husain with his brothers said to have left for Madina on 1st. Survey parties ashore 7 a.m. . . . southern party proceeded via camp to extremity of palms. . . . A shaikh with toothache and no knowledge of the water arrived and with difficulty persuaded to carry out his function of going in front of survey officers to explain [their presence] to people. Some trouble in going through village . . . Nuri appeared near No. 1. position and was told things most unsatisfactory. One well, said to be best, examined and samples taken. Temperature –*very* hot. Party returned to ship. Southern party obstructed and warned by [Arab] officer and escort that they could not proceed north of palm trees. Work done will probably suffice. *Fox* arrived 3 p.m.

4 October. Hardinge arrived. Turks said to be attacking Bir Abbas.

To Wilson Jiddah, 4 October: Telegram
Reported Turks commenced attack on Bir Abbas two days ago. Strength and intentions entirely unknown. Faisal was at Bedur near Khaif yesterday with greater part of his army. A ship going to Buraika for next few days to facilitate communications for Faisal. Sixty camels sent here two days ago with supplies and a *sambuq* to go shortly. Faisal does not intend to fight decisive action. I strongly recommend that Abdullah should come here in case Turkish advance serious. Otherwise Arab forces can concentrate nowhere. Ali Bey asks when he may expect

any QF mountain guns. One battery he says promised long ago and three more asked for by you 22 Sept.

On the same day he sent another telegram to Wilson from HMS *Fox*, telling him of the findings of the 'water search' party. Six main wells had been found altogether, and an almost unlimited supply of brackish, warm water was available along the west-running wadi for about a mile inland, at a depth of about 12 feet, and about $3\frac{1}{2}$ miles from aerodrome site.

5 October. Telegram from Wilson – flight leaving today or tomorrow – dated 4th. Went with Boyle and Perry to investigate landing possibilities. Decided to blow channel in reef to shore and put up shears to hoist packages [crated supplies]. Hurried to post completed report by *Lama* which was to leave next morning – towing *sambuq* – on way to Yanbo. *Dufferin* left 4.15. Arab soldiers and officers (escort) did not arrive.

Four months had now passed since the formal declaration of the Arab Revolt, and still the British officers sent to the Hijaz to help the Sharif and his four sons met with indifference, inter-family wrangling and frustrating inefficiency. Parker's lengthy report addressed to Arab Bureau, Cairo, aboard HMS *Dufferin* 5 October 1916, went over all the ground covered by his diary since his arrival with the Admiral at Jiddah on 26 September. It concluded with a summary of the Rabegh situation, its facilities and the attitude of the tribesmen, townsfolk and the local commander, the Sharif Ali Bey:

Harbour: Good, with room for seven or eight ships to use excellent anchorage.

Landing: Facilities for landing can be made readily. Given the necessary materials and labour three weeks would suffice to prepare a wharf for a ship to come alongside the reef with 24 feet of water. A small jetty for landing stores or men from *sambuqs* or ships' boats could be prepared in three days. A 'K' lighter could be used practically without preparation.

Camping-grounds: With aerodrome on either of the sites near the shore, the camping-ground for the escort would be found on the low coral plateau of the winter aerodrome. Room for any number of men. There is a good site for a brigade camp, landed to defend the Wadi Rabegh south of the fort; the ground is hard, high and gravelly. Ground round the fort much fouled by the present Arab encampment, but there is unlimited space southwards.

Roads: If using the corraline plateau a road about 1,500 yards long may be necessary over the intervening muddy flats in winter, if sea rises. Another road would probably be necessary for Brigade camp, especially if motors [automobiles] were to be used. Material available, corals from reefs. Ground surface passable for light vehicles at present.

Water: Telegram already sent regarding water which is of great quantity but indifferent quality. Could be used for washing and perhaps for cooking, and in emergency for drinking (subject to medical opinion). New wells would have to be sunk and guarded from contamination.

Labour: Probably not available.

Camels: Up to 500 can perhaps be supplied by arrangement with Sharif Ali.

Defensive position: The defensive position at Rabegh runs due east and west along the nothern edge of the palms bordering the Wadi Rabegh. Hidden lateral communications behind the palms. Site for camp roughly in rear of centre of position south of the fort. Water supply immediately in rear of position. Open flat hard plain in front of position extending for several miles except for a promontory of low sandhills stretching about 300 yards from the left of the position. Left flank of position covered by ships' fire at 5,000 yds. Plain in front of position good hard going for armed cars. Passage to front for cars from centre of position, north of fort, if a length of 200 yds of light sand dealt with immediately behind position; or round right (eastern) end of palm trees, where some work would be required across the wadi bed. Two battalions in front line with two in reserve, armed cars to protect flight, and ships' fire on left front should ensure the position against attack by any force the Turks can bring (estimated at one division as maximum).

Climate: More bearable and less damp than Jiddah. From now on

British troops could be sheltered in tents, huts unnecessary. There are said to be mosquitoes, but inhabitants are said not to suffer from malaria.

Supplies: Sheep of good quality probably procurable by arrangement. Also fish. Otherwise nothing.

Military and political: The attitude of the inhabitants, and troops, appears to be thought by Ali Bey to be fanatically adverse to the sight of Englishmen. No signs apparent. There is no doubt that Ali is entirely genuine and entirely grateful for British help. . . . The military situation is not good at present. With Faisal north, and Abdullah entirely out of touch . . . Rabegh cannot be reinforced by other formed bodies of Arabs and if attacked by a Turkish division would probably be captured. Nuri Bey is overwhelmingly confident that he can defend the position given another battery of QF mountain guns. Arabs are not likely to make a good defence in entrenchments and it is difficult to understand Nuri's attitude. Possibly he may be aware that the Turkish forces at Bir Abbas are unimportant, but I do not think this is the case. Otherwise he is over confident and does not wish to share the credit of defeating the Turks, or wishes for their success. I am at a loss. Argument arises out of a conversation yesterday in which he [Nuri] stated that he did not want Abdullah's force to come here as he was sufficiently strong without it. However, I wired to Col. Wilson suggesting Abdullah should come here in case Turkish attack serious and Ali has taken the hint, conveyed via Nuri, and done the same. . . . The telegraph announcing the departure of the flight has been received and it is therefore unnecessary for me to repeat arguments which otherwise I should have elaborated in this report. I have written in very great haste and regret if report is not clear. I attach reports of other officers of the party.

A C Parker, Lt. Col.

The report[16] reached GHQ on the 6th and was transmitted to 'Master' Wingate in Cairo immediately.[17] Even the sanguine Sirdar was alarmed and promptly wired the CIGS in London, by-passing Murray, seeking permission to send a military mission to the Hijaz under Col. Newcombe. Lawrence, still beavering away at maps in the Savoy Hotel was reading the telegrams and reports of Parker and Wilson avidly as they arrived from the Red Sea ships, and doubtless made known to Newcombe his keenness to taste action in the Sharif's cause. The officers on the spot were equally anxious to escape, especially Bray[18] who was attached to Parker though officially Wilson's intelligence officer, and who had already asked to be allowed to return to the relative order and quiet of the Western Front. By the 10th, Parker's report had reached the Foreign Office, already under pressure from India to drop the entire Sharifian escapade.[19]

6 October. Off Abiyad at 8 a.m. Landed with Capt. Boyle, Bannatyne and Malone [relinquished command of East Indies Squadron seaplanes in May, now in charge of planes aboard *Anne* with Capt. Weldon]. Flying ground near heel of promontory found satisfactory. No good landing, and ship cannot get inside toe. . . . Place may do as advanced landing only, ship bringing up requisites before hand. Left at 4.30 p.m. to return to Rabegh. Faisal's agent did not come on board though asked to.

7 October. Arrived Rabegh 8.30 a.m. Perry on shore blowing channel in reef. Transferred to *Hardinge* at 2 p.m.

Parker to Wilson (Jiddah), 7 October: Telegram
Following for Arbur: Ras al Abiyad reconnoitred on 6th. Its employment as permanent Flying Corps base not practical from naval point of view . . . decided that Abiyad can be used as temporary advanced fuel depot in calm weather, thus lengthening planes' radius of action from Rabegh.

8 October. Nuri Bey came on board. Was informed that ship could not be kept at Baraika on account of distance from shore, bad anchorage etc. . . . News that Turks seized Bir Abbas and as far south as pass, on 6th. Regs. 130th, 42nd, and mixed. Also Regt. of two battalions. Artillery. A regt. of cavalry and camelry and three aeroplanes – one already broken and two have not yet been in the air.

Telegrams: to Wilson, 8 October
1341. [After repeating diary detail of Turkish occupation of Bir Abbas:]

Ali Bey asks that mountain batteries be expedited, and barbed wire. Ali informs me that Abdullah Bey leaves Mecca today for Rabegh.

1340. Reported that Husain of Rabegh with 68 followers surrounded by Harb tribesmen. He asked them to approach saying he was loyal to Sharif, and then fired on them inflicting many casualties. His party later attacked by Arabs who wounded one slave and captured some camels carrying rifles. Last news – Husain proceeding Eastwards.

2202. Following from *Dufferin,* Yanbo. Faisal reported to be now at Hamra between Khaif and Bir Abbas. Shaikh Asaaf reports he has blown up bridge of Mala, 24 of the spans being destroyed and the remaining eight damaged. Also he has destroyed the rails for about two miles near Bewat and Ghozail for a distance of 48 telegraph posts. He asks for more gelignite and red fuses. Am proceeding to visit Hassani returning to Sharm Yanbo a.m. 10 October. [Sent 9 October. Meanwhile, remains at Rabegh.]

Telegram: Parker to Wilson, 9 October
2110. *Following for Arbur.* Opportunity for officers with me return Egypt. . . . Bannatyne should also go back if flight not coming. Please instruct me not later than Tuesday evening.

Telegram: Wilson to Parker, 9 October
267. Sharif has asked for Egyptian troops to be landed at Rabegh at once if any available, also British Brigade to be kept ready for instant despatch to Rabegh if situation demands their presence. Sharif has delegated onus of asking for British troops to Ali Bey whom Sharif is instructing to tell you if and when British troops are required. On receiving request for British troops from Ali please wire Arbur urgent direct and inform me. What is present situation of Faisal?

Telegram: Parker to Wilson, 9 October
1535. Reported that on 7th or perhaps 6th Faisal retook Bir Abbas and the Safra defile to south after twelve hours' fighting. Turks retired on Bir al Raiq near Bir Masaid losing twenty killed. Faisal took some prisoners and is following up. Please inform Arbur.

9 October. Parties to shore. Bannatyne, Bray and self to left flank with ten or twelve Sharifian regulars and Hilmi Effendi [one of Ali's Egyptian officers]. Boyle, Brigstocke, Bluitt and two signalmen with helios to ground behind camp. Latter party find some obstacles put in way by Ali Bey, whom Capt. Boyle called on. First party on deciding to return through palms along Sultani warned by Hilmi Effendi to proceed round East end of palms. Refused. Ali Bey interviewed. Strong protest at such rudeness. Ali replies that communications must be without intermediary. Agreed. [Parker and his men did not know at this time that Ali, the tall thin Sharifian prince was in fact consumptive, a condition which no doubt led to his changeable fits of temper and mood.]

10 October. Trials of new pier. Two lifeboats lashed together with platform carrying three-tine anchor towed in and brought up to pier without difficulty. Lunch with Boyle, Nuri Bey and young officer, and Perry. Sketch map found incorrect.

On 7 October Parker had begun another long report to the Arab Bureau in continuance of his report of the 5th. It was another recital of the technical problems of accommodating a land-based flight at Rabegh, of the need for a trustworthy escort of British army men to protect an aerodrome, preparing the harbour and jetty for the influx of vessels and goods which would be necessary, and the difficulties of dealing with the Sharif's obstinate and unpredictable sons. The Sharif was still adamant that Parker could not appoint agents in his territory, so that he was entirely dependent on news received from Sharifian sources. He was not able to dispatch this latest appraisal until the 10th:

The military situation in the neighbourhood of Faisal's army appears to be developing [he noted]. News is extraordinarily scarce, almost non-existent, and it seems impossible to get any information as to the importance and strength of the new Turkish advance on Bir Abbas. Some of Faisal's men appear to have been engaged and he is reported to be proceeding in person to gauge the situation. I understand that if the Turks attempt to advance on Yanbo, he will oppose them at Hamra, while if their objective is to move south down the Sultani road he will not force them to decisive action, but will remain on their western flank and harass them and their communications. It is impossible to guess Turkish intentions without a particle of information as to their strength or transport arrangements. I am endeavouring to inspire Ali Bey and Nuri with the necessity of good, freshly gathered information.

Then there was the problem of Abdullah and his reluctance to join up with his brothers.

One reason against Abdullah coming to Rabegh is I understand that his army is composed of Bani Ataiba [tribes] while all Ali's men are Ha'rb, and though the two tribes have officially buried the hatchet for the duration of the war there is likely to be trouble from their too close contiguity. While in blank ignorance, it is impossible to recommend or suggest any other operations, but I still consider that operations carried out against Wejh and other northern coastal towns are most important in giving the Turks a feeling of insecurity as to their communications. From the last story I heard from those parts, Basri Pasha [Civil Governor of Madina] was likely to proceed to Wejh to keep Arabs sympathetic.

In a postscript dated 10th October, he reported:

On the 8th Nuri Bey came aboard [*Hardinge*, to which ship Parker had transferred on the previous day] and reported the capture by the Turks of Bir Abbas and the Safra defile to the south of it. In view of the apparent possibility of a Turkish advance on Rabegh he emphasised the need for the quick despatch of the QF mountain batteries previously asked for.

He is able to provide a detailed account of the Bir Abbas operations following Nuri's visit:

On the 2nd and 3rd October the Turks approached Bir Abbas and returned under cover of fire from mountain and machine-guns. . . . On 5th and 6th the Turks again attacked with field and machine guns and seized Bir Abbas. . . . On the 7th they appear to have again abandoned [Bir Abbas and the Safra defile] after twelve hours' fighting, retiring to

Bir al Raiq and Bir Masaid, withdrawing their guns with difficulty. Said to have lost twenty men killed besides rifles and tents and some men taken prisoner. According to reports none of Faisal's main body were involved in operations, which were undertaken by Bedouin. Faisal has now sent 1,500 Bedouin to attack Turks at Masaid and intends to move his Egyptian artillery and main body to Bir Abbas and to hold that place. Turkish prisoners give composition of force as: 130th Regt., 42nd Regt., mixed Regt. of Madina locals, Regt. of two batteries artillery, mixed cavalry and camel corps, three aeroplanes. There is no confirmation of the rumoured presence of Kress von Kressenstein at Madina. Information received here is scarce and vague. It is practically certain that the movement on Bir Abbas was not intended as a serious advance, and it seems likely that it may have been meant to draw the Arabs into a position in which they can be engaged to advantage. The destruction of part of the railway by Shaikh Asaaf [Howaitat shaikh, killed on the way to Wadi Sirhan with Lawrence in July 1917] has been reported. It is most important to encourage the Arabs to recognise the importance and feasibility of such action. News received 10th that there is a force of 400–600 Turks with 1,200 Arabs at Wejh and Sharm Habban. The importance which the Turks attach to these places can be readily understood, and the corresponding advantage of transporting a sufficiently large force of Arabs by sea and landing them, provided the situation in the south is assured, is obvious.

There was another plea for a British brigade at Rabegh, and further discussion of the role of aircraft; and an assertion of the need to make a sufficient show of force to bring over to the Sharif the large number of Arabs in the Hijaz who were wavering or actively helping the Turks. And finally: 'One obstacle is the Arabs themselves, and it [an active campaign] should not be undertaken unless they [the Sharif's sons] are completely in agreement and fully comprehend the objectives.'

11 October. HMS *Fox* left for Jiddah and Aden. Bray, Perry, Bannantyne and Brigstocke aboard. Ali Bey, Nuri Bey and two (Arab) officers came on ship at 8.30. Also Sharif Shakir [cousin of the Sharifian princes and Abdullah's No. 2]. Ali again asked for mountain batteries and for motor cars. Nuri asked for Jafar Pasha [the Senussi officer captured by the British force in the war on Egypt's western frontier in February 1916, and an old friend of Nuri's in their native Baghdad and the Turkish army], and for a prismatic compass. Rumoured night attack by Faisal's Arabs, said to have taken 100 prisoners. No water at Bir al Raiq, which is said to be within artillery range of Bir Abbas. Ali apprehensive of Um Lejj. Ali breakfasted aboard and went on tour of ship [*Hardinge*].

On the 12th Parker with one of the survey team, Bluitt, and Nuri and Shakir remained ashore, inspecting the right flank of Ali's Arab army at Rabegh. They were picked up in the late afternoon by HMS *Northbrook*.

13 October. HMS *Hardinge* left for Yanbo and Jiddah. 14 October. Ali and Nuri call in afternoon with news that Faisal has surrounded two Turkish posts at Bir al Ruhi. News received that three ships bringing flight immediately.

15 October. Pacing out ashore to check map.

16 October. Working on pier arrangements on *Northbrook*. Abdal Rizzaq Effendi [Egyptian surveyor] came aboard with map of left front of Turkish position. Afternoon, wire from Wilson that Sirdar did not wish flight to be landed and was communicating with C-in-C Egypt. Reply sent that failure to land flight here after arrival would result in entire loss of faith in our intentions, and that Ali and Faisal had been informed.

Telegrams were flying thick and fast between Rabegh, Jiddah and Cairo at this time. The increasing demands of the Arab commanders, the aircraft question which was still being debated while their carriers *Georgian, Al Kahira* and *Belle View* were on their way from Suez, and the inclination of the Rabegh Arabs to take pot shots at Parker and his men, gave rise to such a flurry of telegraphic messages that several were lost in transmission and had to be repeated. Since the cipher clerks had forgotten to number several of them the repeats were often, and surprisingly, incongruous.

Parker to Wilson, 11 October
Strongly recommend with view to improving communication of news despatch to Rabegh one motor car suitable for desert work with capable Moslem volunteer chauffeur for trial on Sultani road. Anticipated it will be able to run to Bir Abbas.

Wilson to Parker, 11 October
278. Your 1130 of 8 October not clear. What is number of my tel. you wish repeated. Have you received my 267 of 9th. Your 2201 repeated and sent to Arbur. Please quote number of my tels in replying to them.

Parker to Wilson
Your 278. Tel. I asked repeated not numbered. Began 'High Commissioner wires. . . .'

Wilson to Parker, 13 October
Tel. 256 was as follows. Begins – High Commissioner telegraphs that in view of telegrams from you and myself aeroplanes not being sent until urgently required. Please wire if you recommend immediate despatch or not.

Wilson to Parker, 13 October
W.298. Boyle and Bray inform me still trouble about going to Arab positions. I sent strong message to Sharif this morning and orders being sent to Ali . . . to say you are to be allowed to go anywhere within gun range of Arab positions. . . . Please inform if any further trouble.

Wilson to Parker, 13 October
W299. Please give the following to Ali Bey to send to Faisal from Sharif. Begins – 'We thank you after God and all your men for the great services you are rendering.'

Wilson to Parker, 15 October
Just heard that aeroplanes arrive Rabegh between 16th and 18th.

Parker to Wilson, 15 October
Your 317. Turton [Cmndr] had message last night re. aeroplanes. Faisal

Bey writes he has surrounded two Turkish posts at Bir al Ruhi. He is displeased with Egyptian artillery. Reports Turkish planes flying over his camp and asks for our aeroplanes to reassure his Arabs. Ali Bey suggests flying officer making trip by land to Bir Abbas to examine country and I have suggested I go too. Please obtain Cairo approval in case plan goes through.

Parker to Wilson, 15 October
Following for Arbur. Ali Bey asks for motorcycle in addition to motor car already asked for. Strongly recommend one be sent for trial. Riad al Mahairi now on leave can bring when he returns to Rabegh [al Mahairi one of Egyptian survey officers with party].

Parker to Wilson, 15 October
Following for Arbur, subject to your approval. Ali Bey continually asks if mountain batteries are being sent. Can I give him any reply. Are you sending a motor car.

Wilson to Parker, 16 October
Sirdar wishes you notify OC Flight on his arrival that pending further instructions he is not to land and that Sirdar is communicating with C-in-C Egypt with regard to its disposal.

Parker to Wilson, 16 October
12 midnight. Trust matter of aeroplanes will be settled immediately – Ali Bey and Faisal Bey have both been informed of date of arrival. If flight is not landed it must result in entire loss of faith in our intentions.

As the three carrier ships made their way down the Red Sea, the War Cabinet in London met (14 October)[20] to consider once more the question of involvement in the Hijaz; and it was also occupied by loudly voiced French protests emanating from Col. Bremond's mission at Jiddah that the Sharif's ambitions were turning increasingly towards Syria. Britain and France had already signed a secret agreement,[21] negotiated in tandem with their Russian allies, which carved up the Ottoman Empire between them, giving Constantinople to the Czar, Mesopotamia to Britain and Syria to

France in the form of areas of direct rule and areas of influence. That agreement cut across the letter and spirit of the promises made to the Sharif while the so-called Sykes–Picot discussions were taking place. Now France was determined to prevent a Sharifian incursion into Syria. As long as the main Turkish force remained bottled up at Madina and Maan, key points on the Hijaz railway, there was no possibility of a major breakthrough by the Arab army, especially if Nuri Shalan the paramount chief of the powerful Anaiza tribes which controlled the Syrian desert remained loyal to the Turks with whom he had conducted a love–hate affair for many a year. Eight days before the Cabinet meeting of the 14th the War Office instructed Cairo to send a new military mission to the Hijaz, and Storrs, Britain's chief negotiator, was sent on a second journey to Jiddah to talk to the Sharif.[22]

In an atmosphere of growing intrigue and rivalry, the Sharif had decided on 13 October to issue a new proclamation addressed to the people of Iraq, or Mesopotamia as the outside world then knew it, demonstrating his self-enacted leadership of the Arab peoples. On the same day Wilson had told the Arab Bureau[23] of the continuing difficulty of 'getting the Sharif to stick to one proposal'. On that day too, Storrs and his favourite companion of the Arab Bureau, his 'little genius'[24] T. E. Lawrence, left for Jiddah.

The articulate, arrogant, diminutive prince of the Arab Revolt was on his way at last, after an impatient year and a half in Cairo as the catalyst of the Sharifian party in the Savoy Hotel and the High Commission, and occasional editor of Hogarth's *Arab Bulletin*, chronicling the events of the desert war from afar.

7
The New Regime

> I had believed these misfortunes of the Revolt to be due mainly
> to faulty leadership, or rather to the lack of leadership, Arab and
> English. So I went down to Arabia to see and consider its great
> men. The first, the Sharif of Mecca, we knew to be aged. I found
> Abdullah too clever. Ali too clean, Zaid too cool. Then I rode
> up-country to Faisal, and found in him the leader with the
> necessary fire, and yet with reason to give effect to our science.
> So I returned pleased and confident to Cairo.
>
> T.E. Lawrence, *Seven Pillars of Wisdom*

Thus Lawrence began, immodestly, to tell his version of the story
in the eighth chapter of his tale. Even the first page contained a
conversational invention, a learned musical discussion between
Storrs his companion aboard HMS *Lama* on the voyage to
Jiddah, and Aziz al Masri the deserter from the Ottoman army
who had come to take charge of the Sharif's forces. Aziz al Masri
was already in the Hijaz, awaiting the new arrivals. But Lawrence
told a colourful and shrewd story and if it was sometimes too
subjective to be relied on absolutely, or if it was remiss in matters
of detail, it was and will ever remain the most readable account of
the war in the desert.

He may be forgiven a great deal for his account of the Princes of
Mecca and the architecture of Jiddah, of Abdullah's appearance
on his white mare/'through the silent respectful salutes of the
town', of the captured Turkish band which Abdullah brought
with him to dinner at Col. Wilson's house, and which entertained
the guest with a stirring rendering of *Deutschland ueber Alles*,

followed by *Eine feste Burg*, and a 'Hymn of Hate' which nobody recognized. 'Curious the party was,' remarked Lawrence of their meeting on 17 October. 'Abdullah himself, Vice-President *in partibus* of the Turkish Chamber and now Foreign Minister of the rebel Arab state; Wilson, Governor of the Red Sea Province of the Sudan, and His Majesty's Minister with the Sharif of Mecca; Storrs, Oriental Secretary successively to Gorst, Kitchener and McMahon in Cairo; Young, Cochrane and myself, hangers-on of the staff; Sayid Ali, a general in the Egyptian army. . . .Aziz al Masri, now Chief of Staff of the Arab regular army, but in old days Enver's rival.' While Parker waited for Abdullah's Taif force to come down to Rabegh in the face of an expected Turkish invasion from Madina, its general was occupied in high politics at Mecca. Lawrence, who himself gives no dates for his early journeys in the Hijaz, says simply that he left Jiddah 'next morning' for Rabegh. It was the 18th.

17 October. Georgian arrived 10.30 a.m, and *Belle View* afternoon. Maj. Darell, Col. Turner, Bannatyne and [ship's] Captain ashore in afternoon where they saw Nuri Bey and doctor, who asked for a prescription to be made up for Ali Bey who has gastric fever. One hold of *Belle View* on fire. Water may have destroyed stores. Damage so far unknown but likely to destroy efficiency of flight as propellors are there [among stores]. Planes and tenders are elsewhere. Origin of fire supposed to be spontaneous combustion in coal bunkers. News from north that Fakhri Pasha and Basri Pasha have left Madina, perhaps to view damage to Railway.

Wilson to Parker, 17 October
332, 10.30 a.m. I have forwarded your 07 to Sirdar, who is now in charge of military operations Hijaz [the WO had instructed GOC Egypt on 4 October that 'all assistance to Sharif' now in hands of Sirdar].[1] British Govt. has decided that no British troops are to go to Rabegh. Sirdar in his tel. 453 wishes you to notify OC Flight aeroplanes no longer required for Rabegh and must therefore return to Suez. Wire when Flight leaves.

Parker to Wilson, 17 October: 010. Your 332 received and communicated

Sharif Hussain and the map of Arabia: a propaganda device adopted in 1916. From Amin Rihani's Around the Coasts of Arabia, *Constable, 1930*

Northbrook. Georgian and *Belle View* arrived and are remaining until morning pending orders naval CinC.

Parker to Wilson, 17 October: 011. Fakhri Pasha and Basri Pasha said to have gone north from Madina. . . . Some troops also said to have gone north to guard railway or for ops. towards Egypt.

18 October. Georgian left at 10.30 a.m. Nuri Bey arrived and said Ali Bey very ill during previous night, temp. 40 degrees C. Situation regarding aeroplanes explained to Nuri. Telegram that Aziz was to arrive the following day. Also *Arethusa* with stores. Letter sent to Nuri informing him.

On 17th Parker had filed a report to the Arab Bureau confirming the information in his telegrams and diary and noting: 'The withdrawal of the aeroplanes *after* the appearance of the ships in the harbour will make things very difficult.' On the 19th he continued to Arbur with news of Ali and of the breaking to the Arab leaders of the even more serious news of the aeroplane fiasco.

18 October. Nuri Bey came aboard in forenoon. He had been asked the previous day to send horses for Capt. Turton and myself if Ali Bey had been well enough to see us, and if not to come to us himself in the afternoon. He stated that Ali Bey was very ill and unable to see us. He was therefore informed of the immediate return of the aeroplanes to Suez. The doctor and I rode to the camp [Ali's] and the patient was seen in consultation with Mumir Effendi the Arab army doctor. The illness appeared to be an attack of fever with slight bronchial business and Ali agreed to come and sample the ship's fare for a few days. He seemed to appreciate the interest shown.

19 October. Lama arrived with Storrs and Lawrence aboard. Storrs to breakfast and said War Council had decided that British troops not to land in Hijaz; also as to direction [partial] of policy by Sirdar. Aziz also arrived and went ashore with Nuri later. Aziz and Ali Bey had received

العدو ونزل وادي الصفرا من جهتين من علوه ومن

ا و طه من النفيه ولان سيرد وقوة ا هينا ريد

والظاهر انه ظن بانه لقو التي من سنة عا الشرق

السالى ويريد قطع سافتنا اما على البحر او على وادي ينبع

وحيث انني لم اعلم عن حال الغر وتخمينه فانه صح ذلك

وايت والزم ما تركو على رابغ فانتم اشو علم على

الملف وعلى كل .. الغر ودهرب الذي بطرفكم امروهم

يقدمو على كلا متا ليكونون مقدمة جيوشكم وعن

ننظرع ناحتى تنكشف لنا الحاله وامرنا هينا ريد

بانه يسحب الى النبيل

_____

From Faisal to Aly bey

The enemy came down to Wadi el Safrah from two sides El Alwa & Shufia via El Wasta to threaten the force of our brother Zeid. It seems that he thought that my force went to the North East & he wants to cut our rear-guard either to the sea or to Wadi Yanbo & as I know nothing about El Gar situation, I think if they don't move towards Rabegh you should confront

Letter from Faisal to his brother Ali, October 1916

messages from Faisal Bey saying that he found himself hard pressed and that the Turks had received considerable reinforcements. Ali Bey remained on board all day. He was informed of decision of British Govt. re British troops. Lawrence gave information that 800 French troops [Muhammadan] are due at Rabegh about middle of November with one

Rabegh Diary.

19ᵗʰ October. H.M.S Lama arrived with Captain Lawrence, Mr. Storrs and Aziz Bey. Mr. Storrs left immediately for Suez in Golden Crown.

Sherif Ali Bey remained on board all day.

Aziz Bey and Nuri Bey, who had come on board to meet him, went on shore early to inspect —

20ᵗʰ October. Sherif Ali Bey went ashore in morning. Captain Lawrence went with him, and spent the day ashore.

21ˢᵗ October. Aziz Bey and Nuri Bey came on board in morning. The former explained his plan of organizing a force and handed in his list of requirements.

Captain Lawrence left in the afternoon for Sherif Feisal Bey's Camp.

On the 22ⁿᵈ October I paid a visit to Ali Bey and had a long talk with Aziz Bey. He was obviously much dissatisfied with the present state of affairs. He had found things very difficult at Mecca; and at Rabegh he was finding obstacles in the carrying out of his plan energetically. No sooner did he commence trying to obtain volunteers for the so called regular force than he found Ali Bey made difficulties of tribes being split up.

I hope things ~~may go but~~ he may find things go better shortly. He likes Ali Bey and I hope the latter will realize that he must give Aziz a free hand if he is to be of any use.

The advent of the French detachment Aziz looked upon with suspicion and was inclined to ridicule it. No doubt he feels it in some sort clips his wings in Syrian schemes he may have in view.

On the 23ʳᵈ October news was received that Feisal Bey had retired towards Hamra. Also that H.M.S Hardinge was to arrive next day with the Egyptian Artillery from Jeddah.

24ᵗʰ October. H.M.S Hardinge arrived with E.A. Artillery. Said Ali Pasha cheerful but remainder of Officers evidently depressed. Sherif Mohsen brought £50,000 for Feisal Bey.

A page from Colonel Parker's Hijaz diary

battery of mountain guns and two companies of machine guns. Question of Lawrence going up to see Faisal broached but not finally settled.

Lawrence's version of that first day at Rabegh makes an interesting contrast with Parker's matter-of-fact account.

'Moored in Rabegh lay the *Northbrook*, an Indian Marine ship. On board was Colonel Parker, our liaison officer with Sharif Ali, to whom he sent my letter from Abdullah, giving Ali the father's "orders" to send me at once to Faisal.' There is an almost suspicious imprecision. Parker was not liaison officer to Ali, but Political Officer to the entire Sharifian force, serving under Wilson, though secretly since Wilson was supposed to have no military function and was known as 'Mister'. And Parker would not have been put to any great trouble in 'sending' Abdullah's letter to Ali. Ali was aboard the *Northbrook* and Lawrence could have handed it to the elder son of the Sharif had he wished. Already Wilson had seen enough of Lawrence to dismiss him as a 'bumptious ass'. Capt. Boyle, the SNO, took much the same view, describing the busy army captain who had descended on him as 'affected'.[2] Ali, according to Lawrence, was 'staggered' by the Sharif's orders but made the best of them and prepared for the Englishman his own 'splendid riding-camel, saddled with his own saddle, and hung with luxurious housings and cushions of Najd leatherwork pieced and inlaid in various colours, with plaited fringes and nets embroidered with metal tissues'. Parker, clearly, was unaware of these gestures. As a trustworthy man, Lawrence added, Ali gave him Tafas al Rashid, a Hawazim Harb tribesman, and his son, as guides to Faisal's camp at Hamra. It was decided on the 20th that he should go to Faisal and report back to Parker.

20 October. Ali Bey and Capt. Lawrence early to shore. Latter returned in afternoon.

21 October. Aziz and Nuri to ship 9 a.m. Handed in list of requirements. Lawrence left for Faisal afternoon. [It was a day's journey, of which Lawrence made much.]

22 October. Called on Ali and Aziz in morning. Football in afternoon.

23 October. News received that Faisal has retired towards Hamra. *Hardinge* due tomorrow with Egyptian artillery.

24 October. *Hardinge* arrived. Said Ali Pasha [Egyptian commander] fairly cheerful. Remainder of officers sad. Unloading throughout day. Horses and mules being landed by motor lighter towed to beach. Sharif Muhsin [cousin of Sharifian princes] came on *Hardinge* with £50,000 for Faisal Bey. Ali informed and sent Abdullah [son of Tafas of the Hawazimi] to take it over and send it off to Faisal.

Letter to Arab Bureau. Rabegh, 23 October

In view of the final decision of the British Government not to land troops in the parts of Arabia regarded as holy it is well to consider the situation anew:

1. The Turks are improving roads and communications south of Madina. They are reported to have increased the 55th, 160th and 42nd Regiments by one battalion each and to have brought all battalions up to a strength of 800–1000 men each. They have a camel corps and a mule corps, an artillery which appears most formidable to the Arabs, and a much feared aeroplane or two. They are well supplied with camels. The Turks have the advantage of cohesion and single command, as well as the custom of defeating Arabs. They have the permanent disadvantage of a very long and vulnerable line of communication – also the temporary disadvantage in an advance of a scarcity of water on the roads south of Madina.

2. The Arabs have an inchoate and fluctuating army of uncertain numbers divided into three commands each somewhat jealous of the others, under a supreme command which has no defined plan of action. They have little artillery, and what guns they have cannot be used effectively without great risk of capture, since they are in co-operation with irregulars lacking formation and discipline. The Arab army has the advantage of mobility and the moral strength of British support. Their disadvantage consists of a lack of cohesion, a lack of common plan and concerted action, and a danger of quick melting away if disheartened.

3. The Turkish troops (three 4-battalion regiments with supplementary services) are echeloned southwards for about 50 miles south and south-west of Madina. The Amir Faisal's army, said to be of a strength of at least 4,000 Arabs, with base probably at Hamra or Khaif, is in contact with them in the neighbourhood of Bir Abbas. Detachments of Sharif Ali's tribesmen watch Turkish posts south and south-east of Madina. Sharif Ali himself is at Rabegh with about 2,000 good men, and some Bedouin. Sharif Abdullah is said to be about to advance up the eastern road from Mecca to Madina.

4. At present therefore, should the Turks make a determined advance on Rabegh, there is little to oppose them, especially as Sharif Faisal's tribesmen are said to be considerably disheartened. (Of this we shall shortly have first-hand information from Capt. Lawrence.) Two considerations may cause the Turks to delay: the first the difficulty of watering a large force until rains shall have fallen; and the second, the anticipation of finding Rabegh held by British troops supported by British ships.

5. Should they disregard the above and advance in force it is probable that they will take Rabegh, and it is conceivable that in the event of Rabegh falling Arab opposition to the Turks may collapse entirely. Shaikh Hussain Mubarak of Rabegh is still in the hills two days east of Rabegh and on a Turkish approach would quickly have a following; there are also, I am told, discontented elements at Mecca ready to aid the Turks.

6. The military situation therefore is bad. There are two means of frustrating a Turkish advance, one by assembling a reliable and more or less disciplined force based on Rabegh to contest an advance and so give heart to the tribesmen in their guerrilla warfare; the other to force the Turks to look to their rear by cutting their communications by the Hijaz railway. But the Arabs cannot be expected to carry out the second seriously unless the first is assured.

7. In a separate communication, lists are forwarded of requirements put forward by Aziz al Masri necessary for the formation of a regular force of 5,000 men to carry out the functions envisaged in the preceding paragraph; and, if these requirements are immediately supplied, and if

Aziz succeeds in obtaining the human material he requires, which appears to be by no means certain, the situation will ease. The greatest speed is essential if the project is to be successful.

8. Should the scheme fail to take shape quickly, the situation is likely to become rapidly worse and British action against the Hijaz railway in the north, which is presumably not precluded by the terms of the decision of HMG, may be necessary to save it.

A. C. Parker

Summary of attached list of requirements, submitted by Aziz al Masri: dated 24 October 1916

4 Batteries (4 guns each) QF mountain guns, French pattern complete with camel saddles to carry them
Ammunition: 1,000 shells per gun
60 Lewis guns with camel saddles to carry two each
Ammunition: 50,000 rounds per gun
4 pack sets wireless arranged for camel transport
5,000 Egyptian army pattern jerseys, khaki
Khaki drill sufficient for 7,000 prs pantaloons
7,000 small portable tents, Turkish pattern
5,000 water bottles
5,000 Sudan sandles
5,000 haversacks
5,000 canteens (Brit. army pattern)
5,000 Green canvas waterproof sheets
5,000 blankets
1,000 long canvas camel water bags
1,000 Fantasses (18 gals. preferred)
200 prs officers boots (Australian pattern preferred)
600 British army iron cooking pots
2,000 entrenching tools
5 Telegraph interceptors
3 Telephone interceptors
Spare parts and tools for armourer's shop
4 specimen Syrian riding camel saddles with stirrups fitted, for trial

Additional list of medical stores attached. The six wooden huts in Rabegh list (sent earlier) should be struck out, also X-ray and thermocautery. . . . It is not suggested that the whole demand is required immediately. Medical equipment for one light detachment, one field hospital, and some stores for the base, will do to begin with. As the organization of the 5,000 men proceeds so can the medical equipment be increased.

The 24th was a busy day. In a lengthy preamble to his list of require-ments, Parker made a request for eight tailors with attendant machinists to come down from Cairo, to make up the khaki drill into pantaloons. As for the wireless sets asked for by Aziz, he observed that the ex-Khedive, now living in Switzerland and working for the Central Powers, had two men trained before the war who were now in the Egyptian telegraph service. Aziz knew of another Arab operator in the Yemen. Arabs could learn to operate the sets he insisted, anticipating an almost certain excuse for not sending them. There was also a letter to Clayton on the same day.

24 October, 1916
My dear Clayton
Things seem to be bad down here just at present, as you will gather from other letters I have written. The impression that Aziz has, and I think he is probably right, is that the Turks are getting ready for an offensive which they may undertake immediately, but which they are more likely to delay until later in the year, perhaps a month or six weeks hence, when water conditions and climate are easier for troop movements. . . . My opinion remains what it has always been, namely that we should land a British force at Rabegh capable of holding it . . . of course action against the railway, if successful, would have the same effect, but it has to be done *before it is too late*. I suppose it is out of the question to ask HMG to change the decision given, though there are good arguments. If so, let's have action as speedily as possible further north where the soil is not so sacred. Aziz is evidently finding things exceedingly difficult and to do good must have a free hand. I will do what I can to help him. Finally, I don't know what you wish me to do myself. I offered to stay here, as Wilson asked me to, and am quite willing to stay if I can do any good. If

Newcombe comes here I daresay you would like him to run things, such as they are, and if you don't want me please say so. Before Lawrence arrived I had been pushing the idea of going up country and had hoped to go up. Don't think I grudge him, especially as he will do it as well or better than anyone. Since he has been gone, Ali has had a reaction on the subject and is not inclined to agree to other trips, also most necessary. Even Aziz is not allowed to go north to look round. If Aziz is to be kept working please wire me that his scheme of the so-called regular 5,000 men is approved, and the date of sailing of Indian prisoners for Rabegh [a reference to Arab prisoners of war who had been detained in India and were now to be sent to the Red Sea and Cairo for re-education and enlistment]. Haste is important. If he (Aziz) knows we are doing all we can he will perhaps go on, otherwise I fear he may chuck. I have not mentioned Indian prisoners before to you as it was in Lawrence's telegram. The Egyptian artillery look very sad.

As ever,

ACP

Parker's letters and reports, as well as his diary, began to reflect growing dissension in both British and Arab camps. Aziz al Masri, whose position as Chief of Staff of the Arab army had only been ratified on the 20th of the month at a meeting of the Sharif's first ministry under the chairmanship of Foreign Minister Abduallah, was threatening resignation four days later. Ali refused to allow Parker to appoint agents still, despite a request from the DMI Cairo. And Wingate was now taking over political as well as military responsibility for the Sharifian affair. On the 20th, McMahon had told the Sirdar that the best arrangement regarding political authority in the Hijaz 'is for you to have *carte blanche*'. Wingate replied: 'I shall consult you on any doubtful point.' But there was to be no consultation. Whitehall, increasingly alarmed by its Sharifian commitment, was taking the customary way out and dismissing its executive functionary. Master Wingate was now in absolute charge and his own favourite sons were taking over. He had little time for Parker and much for Lawrence, for whom he had engineered the Order of the Nile (for map work) in September.[3] It was now his wish that Newcombe should come down in Parker's place, taking charge of railway demolition in particular, while Lawrence was left to deal with Faisal. Clayton, who had often been the victim of Wingate's inconsiderate attitude to his Staff, was not a man to engage in public or private debate with his superiors and he never defied 'Master'.[4] In any case, Clayton was a keen supporter of the Sharifian cause and Wilson at Jiddah was pleased to be able to deal with 'Bertie' rather than their ultimate chief Wingate.

The next two days' diary entries were intended for transmission to the Arab Bureau: *from Rabegh.*

25 October. The Egyptian Batteries marched off for Arab camp at 7.30 a.m.

26 October. I proceeded to Arab camp and called on Sharif Ali, Aziz Bey and Said Ali Pasha. At interview with Ali I discussed following:

Telephone: The line and instruments having arrived, Ali Bey is to arrange to build a small hut close to the Custom House on beach for instrument placed there for quick communication with ship. Position of other instruments not yet decided.

Intelligence: has at present no organization. Aziz Bey had wished a certain Fariz Bey to undertake it. This has not been decided. I emphasised importance of organizing and broached subject of employing agents of my own and mentioned Hajji Abbas (a Persian). Ali Bey very dubious and pointed out dangers to agents. As regards Hajji Abbas, thought him untrustworthy. (It is obviously undesirable to employ agents unless Ali Bey agrees to principle or failing that to particular persons employed.)

Field Battery: Ali Bey gave me a letter from Lawrence dated 23rd at Faisal's camp and recommending a field battery complete to Yanbo. Without being aware of special arrangements for it I am opposed to project as being unpractical. What is the personnel to be and how trained? The road from Yanbo is unknown to me but the first part of it is almost certainly light sand. (Egyptian guns have traversed it but they are much lighter than field-guns.)[5]

A Field battery could be an enticing objective for the Turks and could not disappear as might mountain batteries on camels. Ali Bey and Aziz Bey agreed that it was preferable to press for mountain batteries.

Visited Egyptian Batteries. Officers pleased to see someone from Egypt. Horses very thin, mules quite good. Said Ali Pasha said he understood it was Sirdar's intention for him to train Arabs in the use of guns and then hand over batteries and return to Egypt [Said Ali could not wait to disengage himself; described Arabs under his command as 'cowardly and undisciplined rabble'].[6] Visited Aziz Bey and have wired gist of his obstacles in getting anything done or obtaining any measure of control, without which his services are useless. On return to ship found that HMS *Raven* had arrived with *no seaplanes on board*. Those on HMS *Anne* are being transferred to *Raven* though *worn out and unserviceable*.

Major Garland arrived in HMS *Raven* and is to commence training an explosive class on 27th. ACP

On the 26th he received a note from Lawrence conveying Faisal's urgent request for a field-gun battery to be sent to Yanbo, the port of Madina, to which he intended to retire, though it was still menaced by Sharif Muhammad Ali's tribesmen. He wrote on the same day to Kinahan Cornwallis who had taken over as Clayton's deputy at the Arab Bureau. Cornwallis had passed on a request from the DMI (Col. Holdich) whose code was 'R'.

Rabegh, 26 October 1916
My dear Cornwallis

Many thanks for your letter. My mails are coming all right now. Hope I was not peevish about them.

As regards R doing intelligence work Madina, how does he propose to do it? As things stand I hold it would be quite wrong to employ agents unless Ali Bey agrees to the principle or to particular agents. Ali would hear of it if I employed agents without telling him, and would be suspicious of it at once.

The situation is bad at present but if Aziz's ultimatum works and he can get moving I think he will do things. Time is a difficulty, as I don't expect the Turks will wait until everything is ready. In conversation, Malone expressed the opinion that it would be feasible for naval

Père Jaussen (centre) French scholar and Dominican priest who worked for Parker in Egypt and the Hijaz.
Photographed at Khan Yunis, 1918.

Sudanese 9th Battalion at Abu Zanima, 1915.

HMS *Diana* and *Nur al-Bahr* off Farun Island in Gulf of Aqaba.

Gurkhas landing north of Tor, led by Parker, 1915; HMS *Hardinge* in background.

Aqaba coastline from Gulf.

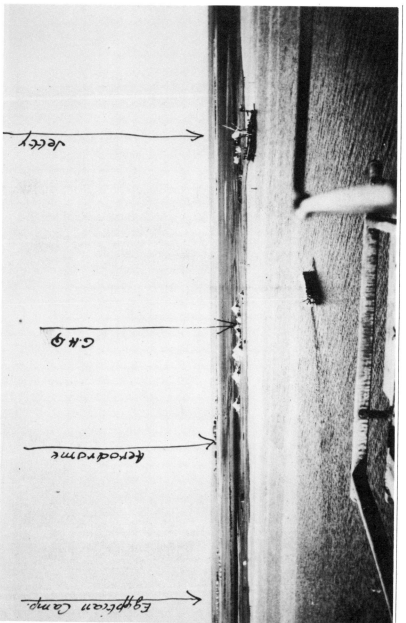

Rabegh photographed from the Red Sea, 1916, showing military installations completed under Parker's supervision. Imperial War Museum.

Reconnaissance flight over Jabal Tubaiq and the north Arabian *'nafud'* (sand dunes). RAF Intelligence photo in Douglas Carruthers collection.

The Amir Faisal's army at Wejh, 1917. Imperial War Museum.

Faisal with *ageyl* troops between Nakhl Mubarak and Yanbo, 1917. Imperial War Museum.

Fakhri Pasha, commander of the Turkish army at Madina, surrenders to the Amir Abdullah at Bit Darwish at end of war. Imperial War Museum.

Colonel S.F. Newcombe with Arab companion in desert.
Imperial War Museum.

Parker and messenger pigeon, al-Arish 1917.

A group of Sinai chiefs at al-Arish in 1924, their photograph sent to Colonel Parker as a Christmas card by the CO: L to R, Shaikh Salama al-Awamra of the Tiyaha, Abu Rabuash, Shaikh Saad abu Nar of the Howaitat, Shaikh Shahuda Daldud of the Tarabin.

aeroplanes to work from a ship, being disembarked and embarked before and after every flight. If this be so the employment of naval aeroplanes does not appear to be subject to the objections put forward to the employment of military aeroplanes. Nor would the use of naval aeroplanes in this way be precluded by the decision of HMG. Perhaps you will discuss the point privately with the Naval authorities. Sharif Abdullah is still loitering in Mecca. I send periodical wires to ask when he is moving north. My opinion is that unless Aziz can be got moving or unless foreign troops hold Rabegh [Col. Brémond was suggesting a French force] or unless Railway is successfully and seriously attacked, there is every chance of a debacle . . . What may possibly hold back the Turks from advancing on Rabegh is their inability to grasp that we can be so foolish as to let them take it if they like.

ACP.

On the 27th a messenger brought Lawrence's second communication from Wadi Safra, a letter dated 24 October written at camp in Hamra.

Colonel Parker

I sent you off a hurried note last night, with a request from Faisal for a field-gun battery. F. is a very impatient general, who is very intelligent, and understands things well. Only I am afraid that some day he will get wild, and spoil the whole show, by trying to go too fast. It's a pity as he is a very nice fellow.

We are sitting at Hamra, which is in a bend of the Wadi Safra. Wadi Safra has about ten fairly large settlements, with water and palm trees, between Bedur and Khaif. It's very jolly here, in a palm-grove with a frame of granite, porphyry, and basalt hills on all sides. The country is incredibly difficult – impossible one might almost say – for movement outside the main wadis. A handful of men who knew their terrain could hold up an army.

For news: not much. Faisal's main force is at Khaif – the same as at Jedida, sitting still. He himself proposes to go to Yanbo al Nakhl and thence to the Railway. The danger is that the Turks have now got their whole force on the Sultani road, and might be let through to Rabegh. By going off towards Hafira he may draw off a third of the force towards

Hamra
Oct. 24.

Colonel Parker

I sent you off a hurried note last night, with a request from Feisal for a field-gun battery. F. is a very impatient general, who is very intelligent, and understands things well. Only I am afraid that some day he will get wild, and spoil the whole show, by trying to go too fast. It's a pity, as he is a very nice fellow.

We are sitting at Hamra, which is in ... of Wadi Safra. Wadi Safra has about ten fairly large settlements. The water and palm trees, between Bedr and Kheif. It's very jolly ..., in a palm-grove, with a ... of granite, porphyry, and basalt hills on all sides. The country is incredibly difficult — impossible one might almost say — for movement outside the main wadies. A handful of men who knew their terrain could hold up an army.

For news :— not much. Feisal's main force is at Kheif — the same as Jedida, sitting still. He himself proposes to go to Yambo el Nakhl and thence to the Railway. The danger is that the Turks have now got their whole force on the Sultani road, and might be let through to Rabegh. By going off toward Hafnie he may draw off a third of the force towards the north, and Abdulla may get as much towards the East. The Arabs will only serve in their districts, so to distribute their forces strengthens them. The Turks on the other hand follow a more normal law! If F. will only go slow for two months, till Egypt is ready, and his own needs better supplies, he may make himself as big as he desires.

We go off to Yambo today :— or at least to Bir Said. I am still counting on reaching Yambo on the 27th, to catch the Lama. It is about 12½ hours actual travel from here, so that I have some in hand. Of course I would like to run across to Nakhl Ibrahim, and so to the port. It does not look as though this would be possible. I am usually introduced as a Syrian officer.

Feisal says he has just had good news from the Billi, who are getting tired of Suleiman Rifada. I hope it is true. Also the Fejir are said to be coming round.

The Egyptians are rather on my conscience: They are on bad terms with the people here. F. has a little A.D.C. Mulud, who is rather a wordy sort of ..., and has ... them. F. himself can find no use for the Egyptian. They turned up at Bir Abbas with their ... guns, and failed to silence a six-inch howitzer. So he turned them down. He wishes he had not got them, and I rather agree with him. If I can persuade him to send them all back to Yambo or Rabegh it will be better, for them and for us. Hussein Zaki Bey is a poor creature; someone with far more strength of mind and drive should be in his place. He only makes fanus fas and

[margin note:] If F. goes off to Yambo before proper steps are taken to replace him here he is running a very serious risk. Ali or Aggyl should move to Bir Hassani before he goes.

the north, and Abdullah may get as much towards the East. The Arabs will only serve in their districts, so to distribute their forces strengthens them. The Turks on the other hand follow a more normal law! If F. will only go slow for two months, till Aziz is ready, he may make himself as big as he desires.

We go off to Yanbo today: or at least to Bir Said. I am still counting on reaching Yanbo on the 29th to catch the Lama. It is about 12½ hours actual travel from here, so that I have some in hand. Of course I would like to run across to Nakhl Yanbo, and so to the port. It does not look as though this would be possible. I am usually introduced as a Syrian officer.

Faisal says he has just heard good news from the Billi, who are getting tired of Suleiman Rifada. I hope it is true. Also the Faqir are said to be coming round.

The Egyptians are rather on my conscience. They are on bad terms with the people here. F. has a little ADC, Malud, who is rather a nosey sort of ass, and has upset them. F. himself can find no use for the Egyptian. They turned up at Bir Abbas with their pop-guns and failed to silence a six-inch howitzer. So he turned them down. He wishes he had not got them, and I rather agree with him. If I can persuade him to send them all back to Yanbo or Rabegh it will be better for them and for us. Hassan Zeki Bey is a poor creature; someone with far more strength of mind and drive should be in his place. He only make(s) *faux pas* and lays himself open to troubles. The tribesmen here seem pretty cheerful. There is a lot of very strong feeling against the Turks abroad!

It took me 26½ hours riding to get here; and Hamra is, I think, a little S.W. of where the 500,000 (WO map) puts it. Total distance 90–100 miles. Yanbo is only about 12 hours camel from here. I have made a number of alterations in the map, though, as we thought, the original traverse of the Sultani road is good. It is the districts off the road that we have got all wrong.

About road surfaces. On the 1/500,000, which you have probably now received (copy to Nuri and Aziz please) you may call the Rabegh–Mastura patch good. The soil is usually shingle like central Sinai, with occasional patches of scrub and blown-sand in hollows. The sand is usually shallow, and could, I think, always be avoided by bearing to E or W. Armoured cars should be able to work from sea-shore to the foothills. The first little hills on parallel 23 are annoying. Cars would probably be able to turn them on the W. They are lava, and the road across the neck, as marked, is stony by nature, and has had cairns added to it. The brush-wood does not give much ground-cover. The 'narrow sandy path' and foothills near Mastura I did not see. A force coming against Rabegh would have to water at Mastura, and there is nothing beyond to Bir al Shaikh. The water at Mastura is small in quantity – in a stone well about 20 feet deep. This might be blown in if a Turkish advance took place. The water supply at Khuraiba should be examined, with a view to possible destruction if necessary. From Mastura northward the hills between the Sultani road and the sea do not exist; that is they are so low as not to be worth marking. The road surface is like that S. of Mastura, only more sandy and more stony patches. An armoured car might do it, and a light car certainly would. It would be slow and bad for the tyres. The hills on the Sultani road at S.U.L.,[7] SW of Bir al Shaikh turn back to a range that joins the T of Sultani to the isolated hill S. of W. of Wadi Safra. The Sultani road goes nearer the T than marked, and then turns E. of Bir al Shaikh. The run down to Bir al Shaikh is soft and sandy, and I don't think a car would do it. At Bir al Shaikh is a brushwood village of the Bani Salem Harb. From Bir al Shaikh to Bir ibn Hussain the road at first mounts a sand slope which would be rather a problem. From the N. of Sultani the surface is good. Bir ibn Hassain (Hassani) I saw at dawn, when it looked splendid. Jabal Subh, which runs on the E. of the road from Bir al Shaikh to Bir al Shofia, is a very sharp and jaggy range of peaks. Wasta is just S. of Kharma, and with Hamra is W. of where we put it. This brings Wasta into W. Safra. S. of Wasta there is the Arab Jedaida. The Turkish Jedaida is called Khaif. So Jedaida should be erased between Hamra and Bir Abbas, and the distance between those places greatly increased. T.E.L.

PS. If F. goes off to Yanbo before proper steps are taken to replace him here he is running a very serious risk. Ali or Aziz should move to Bir ibn Hassani before he goes.

[I have retained Lawrence's spelling of place and personal names, except for 'Yambo' where I have used 'Yanbo' to be consistent.]

With Lawrence's report to Parker, showing something of the

military plan which would be put into effect should it prove possible to land a British force, there was also delivered a message from Faisal to his elder brother Ali.

The enemy came down to Wadi al Safra from two sides, Al Alwa and Shufia via Al Wasta to threaten the force of our brother Zaid. It seems that he thought that my force went to the North East and he wants to cut our rear-guard either to the sea or to Wadi Yanbo and as I know nothing about Al Gar situation, I think if they don't move towards Rabegh you should confront them at Al Milaf and at Kala(t) al Gar. Bid (Bani) Harb who are with you to advance to Kala(t) at once in order to be at your advance guard and I will wait as I am and then we will discover their intention. I bid my brother Zaid to retreat to Al Negail.

Under the Sirdar's stewardship of Hijaz affairs, the Arab Bureau was infused with new life, and the diary from now on consisted of daily reports to the Bureau, with short summaries only for Col. Parker's personal record.

For Arab Bureau, Cairo:
from HMS Suva, *31 October 1916, nearing Yanbo*

27 October. HMS *Suva* arrived Rabegh under command of Capt. Boyle. HMS *Anne* left for Suez same day towing motor lighter. In the afternoon Sharif Ali Bey, Aziz Bey, and Nuri Bey visited ship. Owing to no notice having been given no one was present to receive them on arrival aboard, an omission which was felt by Sharif Ali at the time to be a slight. Subsequent explanations, and requests that notice should be given, have entirely effaced it.

28 October. Capt. Boyle and I visited Sharif Ali Bey and walked round artillery camp, an example of neatness. Some Arabs, probably townsmen, were receiving gun drill instruction which was excellently given by an Egyptian officer, and were showing the greatest keenness to learn. Only news from the north contained in a letter from Faisal saying that he had retired to Bir Said and did not intend to undertake any further operations until both Sharif Ali and Sharif Abdullah should advance.[8]

Said Ali Pasha handed in a report he had received from Bimbashi [Maj.] Hassan Zeki, artillery commander with Sharif Faisal, complaining of the operations he was expected to carry out without assistance or assured support. Said Ali Pasha had added a letter expressing his dissatisfaction with the Rabegh force, with which he might have to operate, and declining responsibility should he have to advance with it to undertake active operations.

29 October. Aziz al Masri came to lunch on HMS *Suva*, to which he had been invited in order to discuss confidentially the manner of his employment with the Arab forces and the best means of removing obstacles by which he found himself confronted.

HMS *River Fisher* arrived from Port Sudan with Sagh Muhammad Effendi Tewfiq, the relief for Bimbashi Hassan Effendi Zakki, and men to replace the time-expired [Egyptian] artillerymen at Rabegh. Also stores and 1,700 boxes small arms ammunition.

On the 30th there was another long essay on the disputed questions of British army assistance, resisted by both the Sharif and the War Office in London, but demanded by Ali; the equivocal position of Aziz Al Masri, nominally in command of the Sharifian forces but unable to make any decisions of consequence; the refusal of Ali to organize a trained infantry force capable of resisting a Turkish thrust or to detail men to dig trenches and fortifications; and the freedom still accorded to Husain of Rabegh to run riot in the rear of the Arab army. A number of suggestions were put forward to Ali when Parker met him at camp at 8 a.m. The Sharif's elder son was told that HMS *Dufferin* had arrived with more reinforcements, two companies of the 6th Battalion Egyptian Army as escort for the artillery. Then:

To all these suggestions Sharif Ali assented, and declared that he would immediately write to his father to approve them. In the afternoon HMS *Suva* left Rabegh for Yanbo and I took passage in her, firstly in order to meet Capt. Lawrence at Yanbo and hear his account of Faisal's army, and secondly to proceed to Jiddah to press the Sharif through Col.

Wilson to give Aziz Bey the powers already described and to assist him in the speedy supply of good recruits.

The diary becomes badly smudged at this point, and the margin contains the note 'Wave through porthole'.

The supply of mountain guns still remains urgent, not so much because they have the power to destroy the enemy, but because the Arabs attach to them an entirely exaggerated value, and therefore find it difficult to take the field confidently without them. . . . The question of bringing suitable Arab prisoners from India direct to Rabegh, there to be offered service in the Sharif's cause, is also most important, since their numbers (estimated at 2–3,000) would immediately make it possible to form the body of 5,000 men already discussed in previous communications, now somewhat in the air with regard to human material. Up till now, no system of intelligence exists, nor should you expect one until Aziz Bey has command, and money to burn, when I anticipate close collaboration with us. Ali Bey, without I think any intention of holding things back, does not pass on the ordinary news he receives. If we can get an officer under Aziz to work solely on this subject the result should be good, especially as it will be possible to check values with Sharif Ali from his knowledge and from the news brought in by his spy system, which no doubt he will continue in any case.

Postcript: Yanbo, 31 October. I have just seen Capt. Lawrence (arrived late on 30th with Abdal Kader, the Sharif's amir at Yanbo), who reports most favourably on morale of Sharif Faisal's army and on the very great difficulties before any Turkish force attempting to advance south from Bir Abbas along the Sultani road. The Arabs have made a fetish of the power of artillery, and their opinion of the Egyptian artillery is low chiefly owing to the latter having failed to carry out the impossible task of silencing long-distance Turkish howitzers. According to Lawrence no aeroplanes have yet flown over the Arabs, though they are reported to be at Bir Darwish. Capt. Lawrence appears to apprehend more danger of a Turkish advance down the Fura'i road or by Khuraiba than down the Sultani. It appears most important that H.E. the Sirdar should have first-hand information of the nature of the country and the situation and

I have therefore advised Lawrence if he can spare the time to proceed to Jiddah and endeavour to obtain a passage, possibly in the C-in-C's ship (*Euryalus*) to Port Sudan, proceeding thence to H.E. This he is doing, Capt. Boyle having been so kind as to offer to take him to Jiddah. ['The aim of my trip was fulfilled,' wrote Lawrence. 'My duty was now to take the shortest road to Egypt with the news and the knowledge gained that evening in the palm wood grew and blossomed in my mind.']

Telegram just received from Rabegh that the Turks have advanced to Bir Hassani and that an advance on Rabegh is threatened. Ali Bey and Aziz request help. I am sending communication to Sharif Faisal recommending him to attack their communications, and am asking Wilson to press for Abdullah's move direct to Rabegh with all speed. I am telegraphing to Ali Bey advising him to call up all his available Arabs and to endeavour to weaken and harass the Turkish advance.

In the personal diary for the 30th, Parker had noted: 'Report that Ibn Saud has seized a certain Ibn Farun' who was on his way from central Arabia to Madina to sell large numbers of camels to the Turks. The diary also noted that, according to Aziz al Masri, the Sharif had treated with rudeness and arrogance envoys sent by Ibn Saud to Mecca. In fact, the Amir of Najd had featured centrally in the political manoeuvres of the Sharif and his son Abdullah during the month. While Abdullah was supposed to be helping to prosecute the war he spent most of the time with his father at Mecca planning moves which would finally bring to an end the career of the unsuspecting McMahon in Cairo, and cause an almost complete rupture at a critical moment of the war between Whitehall and the Viceroy's Government. On 6 October, Ruhi who was then at the Sharif's palace telegraphed Cairo in response to a message from McMahon, that the Sharif regarded Ibn Saud as 'a friend'.[9] Three days before that enquiry, on the 3rd, the Sharif had been shown Britain's hitherto secret treaty with Ibn Saud which had been negotiated by Shakespear at the beginning of 1915 and was signed by Sir Percy Cox and the Amir on 26 December 1915. The Sharif had become increasingly tetchy, issuing on the 13th a 'Proclamation to the Peoples of Iraq', welcoming them as brothers in the 'Arab State'. On the 17th Cox at Basra was told to send a message to Ibn Saud asking him to attack the army of Ibn Rashid in order to assist the Sharif.[10] Within two days of Storrs's conversations at Jiddah, on the 23rd, a Sharifian decree was issued requiring all Ottoman subjects in the Hijaz to register as 'Sharifians' or to leave the country. Britain knew nothing of the decree, which meant that all Arabs, including Najdis, in the holy territory, must declare loyalty to the Sharif; it was transmitted to the Foreign Office by the French Embassy in London. On the 29th, while Parker was on his way to Yanbo, the Sharif's Foreign Minister, Abdullah, dropped a bombshell, announcing that the Ulema and Nobles of Mecca had declared Husain *Malik al bilad al Araby*, 'King of the Arab Lands'. Ibn Saud, whom Aziz al Masri still regarded as the true leader of the Arab peoples, was beside himself with anger according to Cox. So was the Viceroy of India. The Foreign Office, acting as if it had had nothing to do with the negotiations which led to the claim, turned on the unfortunate McMahon.[11]

On 30 October, Wilson had reported to the Sirdar: 'Situation here does not improve and Rabegh force is entirely unready . . . Aziz al Masri has been given no control. . . . He has been trying to get Sharif Ali to approve his various schemes. Latter generally approves in principle and then hinders passively. . . . Have asked Parker if he would like to have talk with Abdullah and endeavour to get Sharif to give Aziz more control.' Meanwhile Wilson sent Bray back to London to see if he could induce the War Office to step in despite Sharifian opposition by sending British [as opposed to Egyptian] troops. Parker left Yanbo on the afternoon of the 31st and was at Rabegh at 8.30 next morning with Lawrence aboard the *Suva*.

1 November. Capt. Warren to ship to say that Ali and Co. would come to ship at 2 p.m. They did so to say that matters had been exaggerated and that 80 *ageyl* [desert gendarmes] had reconnoitred Shufia which had caused rumours. *Suva* left for Jiddah at 4 p.m. with Lawrence on board. I transferred to HMS *Dufferin*.

The latest scare from the Arab front was dealt with more fully in the Arab Bureau daily report:

Sharif Ali had written to Capt. Warren to say that he would visit Capt. Boyle at 2 p.m. His arrival was awaited. On coming he explained, somewhat shamefacedly, that the report had been incorrect and had apparently been based on stories of a patrol of 80 ageyl camel corps which had reconnoitred the northern end of the Shufia defile. (This subsequently boiled down to a party of eight!) Plans were discussed. . . . My suggestion was that Sharif Ali should go north with his camel corps and inspire . . . the Arabs facing the Turks, leaving the greater part of the infantry at Rabegh to continue organising and training. Aziz al Masri favoured the bold plan of moving the Rabegh base bodily to Yanbo and co-operating with Sharif Faisal from there, the presence of the force on their flank being sufficient he suggested to deter the Turks from an advance south. The scheme has the drawbacks that it leaves Husain Mubarak an entirely free hand to canvass the tribes and offers the Turks an open road if they are willing to . . . risk leaving an enemy on their right flank. On the other hand a force at Rabegh entirely unready . . . to defend itself is only likely to be of the greatest danger to itself and to the cause generally. The resulting decision was not clear cut but Sharif Ali stated that he would send some part of his force north and would accompany it himself or send with it Sharif Shakir.

2 November. Visited the Arab camp. Aziz appeared more hopeless of organizing anything in face of constant obstacles. The original plan of the 500 regulars has become to him a Castle in Spain and his intention as now expressed is to form as soon as possible a reliable and mobile camel corps of 800 men, and with them to lead raids on Turkish communications and on the Railway. He feels himself entangled in a mesh of responsibility without control and command without authority and wishes to cut himself loose in however small a way. . . . I visited Said Ali Pasha and, finding that no digging had been done, explained to him that the divided counsels did not absolve him from the necessity of making defensive works immediately, both for his guns and infantry. . . . A telegram from Yanbo reported that Nuri Shalan had driven in a Turkish force near Medain Saleh.

3 November. The Egyptian officers have made good progress with defence works. All Arab officers (ex-prisoners) have resigned owing to ill-judged action by Sharif Ali in punishing one of their number by 24 hours detention for striking a soldier who did not obey order. Aziz Bey on asking Sharif Ali to purchase twenty riding camels was refused. On first rumour of a Turkish advance he [Ali] came whining for British help. During the last month he has done nothing to improve defences except on the morning of the scare. He stands as an impenetrable obstacle to anyone doing it, or to any organisation whatsoever.

4 November. First rain of the season. Sea level has begun to rise considerably and spread over the mud flats round the harbour. I visited Sharif Ali and pressed him to take defence works in hand . . . succeeded in rousing him to show of anger and petulance. He complained that he was not supplied with the necessary batteries of artillery and asked how he could be expected to defend Rabegh without them. I pointed out that the backbone of any defence must be the infantry and if, in the case of Rabegh, the latter were not organised and properly entrenched it made it extremely difficult for me to press for the guns. Finally he promised that the entrenchment work should be completed in five days. With regard to Arab officers I pointed out the necessity of upholding their authority. (They have withdrawn their resignations.) Visited Said Ali Pasha whom I found sadder than usual. Stray bullets had pierced his tents, fortunately without casualties, but the culminating trial was the theft of sandbags, filled and built so carefully during the previous day, emptied and stolen by Arabs during the night. As a matter of fact, indiscriminate firing has decreased greatly. . . . Sharif Ali has sent 100 ageyl [camel corps] to Bir al Hassani. Aziz al Masri, having experienced great difficulty in the purchase of camels, suggested formation of a purchasing board. To this Ali agreed. Maj. Garland has been training men in explosive work at Rabegh, but the men sent to the classes invariably live nowhere near the railway. Sharif Ali agreed that it would be better to send Garland to Yanbo to train classes of Juhaina Arabs and others from railway districts. [Garland, that most courageous of British officers, whose command of Arabic enabled him to teach the Badu to use explosives, suffered from a weak heart though none of the men knew it whom he led in demolition work on the Hijaz Railway. But miraculously the Turks were always able to repair the damage even in the terrible summer heat of the desert, and the line was in service almost to the end of the war, despite the determined work of Garland and, later, Newcombe.]

The diary for 4 November ended on a laconic note: 'Ali Bey informed me that Aziz was in command.'

5 November. Telegram from Col. Wilson that Sharif has decided that Abdullah should proceed by the Eastern road. Also that 700 men and two Turkish guns (captured) were to come direct to Rabegh. Report that Turks have advanced from Ghayer; from report a small local movement of little importance.

6 November. News from Sharif Faisal to Sharif Ali that Arabs have captured convoy of 80 camels.

7 November. HMS *Hardinge* due at Rabegh tomorrow with 6 howitzers, 4 field-guns, and stores. French ship *Pothuau* arrived in afternoon direct from Jiboute. Presumably summoned at time of report of Turkish advance.

8 November. Hardinge arrived 11 a.m. and unloaded stores and guns.

On the 7th the High Commissioner, Cairo, had assured the new Viceroy Lord Chelmsford that neither Wilson nor Col. Brémond had attended the Coronation ceremony at the end of the previous month when Husain of Mecca was crowned 'King of the Arab Lands', though a few days earlier the Foreign Office had instructed Wilson to offer the 'congratulations of HMG'. Wilson was instructed not to use the address 'Your Majesty'. On the 8th, the Foreign Office 'entirely approved' a placatory message from the Resident in the Persian Gulf, Col. Knox, to Ibn Saud.[12] On the same day Maj. Bray arrived in London from Jiddah to seek Sir Mark Sykes's assistance in appealing to the War Cabinet. On the 14th Clayton told Wingate that he would like to keep Lawrence in Cairo, but the Sirdar overruled him. According to Brémond, Lawrence had arrived back at Jiddah on the 3rd.

On 8 November Parker sent another report to Arab Bureau, Cairo, detailing the exact strength of the Arab force at the key point of Rabegh. There were, he said, 3,100 infantrymen and gunners, and 835 of the Camel Corps made up of Ageyls (trained desert guides) and Ataiba tribesmen. Artillery consisted of two howitzers, 13 machine-guns, and three Turkish mountain guns. Recent reinforcements brought in by *Hardinge* and the French ship *Pothuau* had added considerably to the artillery available. Yet before the recent reinforcements of men and guns, Ali had told Parker that he had 5,000 men. '. . . it shows what reliance can be placed on the ordinary statement of fact made by Arab leaders'. As for the immediate danger of a Turkish attack:

From the Turkish point of view it is doubtful if they can afford the numbers to attack Rabegh, with the necessity of guarding the railway and keeping in check the mountain Arabs with Faisal, but I cannot see any impossibility in their doing so. Capt. Lawrence, who has seen the country, I think exaggerates the difficulties. In India it has been proved that provided a force can move quickly enough it can carry out its objective in the face of the opposition of a hill tribe, a more efficient enemy than the Arab. [Finally:] Since writing the above I have received letters from Col. Wilson detailing the plan of operations approved by the Sharif for the three brothers, namely Faisal to remain where he is, Abdullah to move up the Eastern road, and Ali, leaving 2,000 men at Rabegh, to move up on the Fura'i and Sultani roads on the arrival of Abdullah at Hajaria. I discussed the scheme with Sharif Ali today. He found it good, and I trust that he will leave at the time appointed. I shall endeavour to leave Aziz al Masri at Rabegh to organise the defences.

To Arab Bureau, Cairo. In continuation of daily reports, Rabegh 15.11.16

8 November. Sharif Ali visited *Pothuau*, as well as HMS *Dufferin* and *Hardinge*. The Syrian Arab Officer Ahmad Shaika presented to Sharif Ali and accepted into the army. Sharif Ali expressed gratitude at the arrival of the guns (on *Hardinge*).

9 November. Sharif Ali informed that aeroplanes were being sent [his personal diary recorded that planes and escort had arrived already]; also explained that available wireless sets were unsuitable and could not be supplied. Disembarkation of all stores and horses completed by 4 p.m. HMS *Hardinge* left at once for Jiddah. [The War Cabinet had met on the 9th and 10th November to discuss the Arab Revolt and 'a place called Rabegh', with Bray and Sykes in attendance. It was agreed that planes and troops, at the discretion of the GOC Egypt, should be made available for the defence of Rabegh].[13]

10 November. Horses sent to Arab camp last evening to be on beach early morning for saddling. Arrived 10.45 a.m. Saddles fitted and two battalions marched off in some confusion owing to inexperience of Arab drivers at 1.45 p.m. French ship *Entrecasteaux* arrived in morning. Gun tampered with, put right by armourer of HMS *Dufferin*.

11 November. HMS *Suva* arrived with aeroplane escort at 11.30 a.m. 250 Egyptian infantry under command of Maj. Joyce. No tents and 28 fantasses only! *Suva* left for Jiddah 4 p.m. Two limbless howitzers and four-gun howitzer battery handed over and removed, and quantity of shell.

12 November. The British officers with the Egyptian troops [Maj. Joyce and Capt. Davenport, of whom Lawrence was to write, 'The two Englishmen to whom the Arab cause owed the greater part of its foreign debt of gratitude'][14] and self to see trenches by previous agreement, accompanied by Nuri Bey. Ali had promised on the 4th that they would be completed in five days. Interviewed Sharif Ali afterwards and Joyce emphasised necessity of defensive works. Joyce willing, if necessary, to go himself to encourage men in their work. Ali, in reply to another request, refused to allow British officers to see his troops unless orders received from Mecca. He expressed annoyance that he should be doubted, though in what way was not clear. . . . In conversation Ali gave the information that Husain of Rabegh's eldest brother had arrived in Rabegh, and that his only son was expected. Ali thought Ḥusain Mubarak would follow. The staff officer [Egyptian] Mahmud Effendi Hilmi, who had been instructed to visit the camp in the afternoon to

obtain a new return on the troops was met with a point blank refusal. . . .
The French yacht *Al Hadj* arrived with Col. Brémond and Col. Cadi.
Brémond said that Admiral Wemyss had told him the French troops
were required as part of the aeroplane escort. I told him that there must
be a misunderstanding; I understood that the French troops were to
defend Rabegh and not the aeroplanes which already had their escort.

15 November. HMS *Dufferin* left early. A request to Sharif Ali to be
allowed to interview Ismail, brother of Husain Mubarak, met with weak
excuses. Reported that Ismail left on night of 14th with £2,000 for
Husain from Ali. Letter sent to Sharif Ali for Sharif Zaid asking Faisal
questions re. Nuri Shalan's agent and his co-operation with a British air
raid [around Maan]. Sharif Ali in a telegram to the Sharif of Mecca
stated that he had received two boxes [of gold?] from the French. The
French military mission visited Sharif Ali. Site for a camp selected about
4,000 yards NE of Custom House landing place. . . . Col. Cadi in
conversation [said] he had no intention of endeavouring to train any of
the Arab troops, which he considered impracticable. Letter received
from Ali objecting to the flags erected at various points around harbour
for marine survey purposes.

It is impossible to give accurate estimate of the Arab army at Rabegh.
500 Camel Corps have recently arrived and are going with Zaid to Sharif
Faisal. The numbers are therefore about the same as last reported, with
deduction for wastage . . . Sharif Ali's truckling with Husain, if true, is a
peculiarly weak and foolish policy. PS. Sharif Ali has just informed me
that by an arrangement made by him Husain Mubarak was attacked two
days ago and that it is not known whether he escaped or was killed. The
matter (see last secret report) is not clear.

On 16 November HMS *Scotia* arrived from Yanbo with the Sharif
Faisal aboard. Already the harbour was crowded to capacity with
British and French ships. There is a long dissertation on the
brothers Ali and Faisal who began to argue from the moment of
meeting:

Sharif Faisal arrived in HMS *Scotia* with 28 Juhaina shaikhs who are to
be shown all the guns. Sharif Ali and Sharif Faisal met on *Scotia*. The

latter, much angered by Ali's inaction, enquired number of guns and men at Rabegh. Ali defended himself and appeared to assent to an immediate move but theorised over taking French batteries which are still at Suez. I pointed out that it was unlikely that the French would break up their force immediately on landing, and advised that Ali's force should be kept as mobile as possible, since among the mountains it was likely that only a few guns could ever fire at one time to advantage, and the taking of more could be an encumberance. I also advised the leaving of the Egyptian troops, partly since Said Ali Pasha was sick . . . the brothers landed and proceeded to the camp. In the evening I went there to ascertain the result of their discussion. They had evidently quarrelled and made friends and the air was clear. Plans were explained. Faisal to go to Bir Said and establish there the Sharif Zaid, giving him instructions to remain inactive until Ali should arrive near Hassani, where he was to operate. Faisal is then to go up Wadi Yanbo to Khaif Hassan and on his arrival there Ali is to advance from Rabegh to Hassani. Faisal is to take three mountain guns of Ali's. What artillery Ali will take is not yet decided but probably the Field Battery and possibly the Egyptian mountain guns with Arab crews, leaving the Egyptians in charge of the Howitzers at Rabegh. As regards Wejh, there are said to be 1 ½ – 2 battalions of regulars [Turks] there together with 600 Ageyl Camel Corps and some guns. Also Basri Pasha. Sharif Nasir with 2,000 men is on the Billi-Juhaina frontier and an advance will be made shortly reinforced by Faisal's army if necessary, a ship being asked to assist. Suleiman abu Rifada has written a temporizing letter and has been sent a reply that only if he comes himself will his honesty be believed. His own section [of the Billi tribe] have declared themselves willing to leave him if attacked. Faisal now attaches, and rightly, the greatest importance to the capture of Wejh as being likely to bring in the tribes and endanger the railway. . . . Faisal reports the presence of 150 tents at Bewat, 250 at Al Ala and 400 men at Abu al Naim. He expected to be able to distribute another 15,000 rifles in two months' time. . . . He also asked for four armed motor cars, for work northwards from Abu al Naim, should it prove possible to get them to that place. It is refreshing to talk to a man like Faisal after Ali's pettinesses. ACP.

17 November. Sharif Faisal motored down at 5 a.m. I met him and took him out to HMS *Suva* which left at once for Yanbo. Discussion subsequent to my meeting the brothers on evening of 16th had changed plans somewhat, and Faisal is to take two of the field-guns which Ali asks to be sent to Yanbo with 35 horses as soon as possible. Arrangements being made. Aeroplane landing continued. The Crossley motors run easily over the mud flats to the coralline plain. Sharif Ali called in afternoon and met Maj. Ross. Asked for gunnery officer to call and see guns. This had been previously declined. Faisal's visit has put him in a more reasonable frame of mind.

18 November. Sharif Ali spoken to about arrival of Indian prisoners [Arab officers sent down from Indian POW camps] and asked to make detailed plan for their reception. . . . Probably the best course would be reception of officers coming from India by officers at present serving, aboard HMS *Minerva.* Later men to be brought across in batches, the likeliest first, to the *Minerva.* If first part [of plan] successful, parade on shore with band, loyal address etc. Subsequent training of the men as quickly as possible is most important. If Aziz al Masri has returned, they might be handed over to him *en bloc*, subject to Sharif's approval. Otherwise it would be most desirable that they should be given a course of training by British officers and then handed over, but the objections to this in the vicinity of the Arab camp appear unsurmountable. Some [Turkish] prisoners in camp. *Hope* to take statements tomorrow.

19 November. The Batteries marched down to the shore fully manned to explain their requirements in extra horses etc. A list has been sent in. Some of the horses suffering from the heat and it is pretty certain that they could not stand a summer in this climate. I visited camp to see prisoners taken by Faisal's army, and although I had expressly asked Sharif Ali to allow me to interrogate them they had already been sent off to Mecca. All the men were of the 1st Battalion 55th Regiment. The 1st Btn is south of Bir Abbas, 2nd Btn at Khals west of it, and 3rd with HQ at Bir Masaid. 1st Btn complete with transport numbers 800. 130th Regt (3 Btns only) is at Watr and Bir Abbas 42nd Regt (also 3 Btns) is 12 hours off in direction of Ghayer. Two aeroplanes at Bir Darwish, one at Madina. No Germans anywhere. Soldiers have plenty of food and are told that peace will be declared soon. The prisoners were part of a patrol of 17 men near Bir Abbas who were ambushed by Arabs, eight being killed immediately and the remainder taken prisoner.

I am told that Sharif Ali is hurt at the non-recognition [by the Allied powers] of his father's declaring himself 'King'.

20 November. HMS *Hardinge* arrived 8 a.m. to take two 15-pounder guns etc. to Yanbo with 60 Arab gunners and 250 Bishr infantry for Faisal. Message sent to camp for guns, horses etc. Unfortunately, after failing to reply to message last evening for gun practice in morning, Nuri Bey turned up at 9 a.m. with 15 pounders. Range firing not much good. Horses embarked on lighter at 1 p.m. but she went aground and got off late. 250 men embarked (for transfer to *Hardinge*).

21 November. Second loading of horses 8.45–9.15, but lighter did not reappear until 11.45 when last animals aboard and *Hardinge* sailed. Sharif Ali called in morning and visited aerodrome. Aeroplane landing strip finished after six days. Tewfiq Bey, doctor from Aleppo, and Dr Mahmud with four Syrian soldiers arrived. Escaped from Bir al-Mashi.

22 November. Visited camp in motor. Sharif's advance is to take place in 10–15 days – Faisal expects to leave Bir Said in five days. Sharif Ali proposes to leave a battalion of 500 men and 200 Mualid, also Egyptians, in charge of remaining guns at Rabegh. Is wiring father to send Sharif Shakir to take charge at Rabegh. Sharif Ali is writing to Faisal to ask him if he is going to take over Egyptian guns.

23 November. Howitzer and 15-pounder practice in morning. Indifferent but keen. Ali called. Fighting between Somalis (from ships) and Ali's followers. *Al Hadj* [French yacht] arrived. Doctors decide that water unfit for French Muhammadan troops and that they must have distilled water. *Al Hadj* sailed for Suez 2 p.m. with Col. Brémond aboard.

24 November. Examined stores brought by *River Fisher*. Some deficiencies in SAA and boxes containing various items for officers. No packing notes. River Fisher left at 2.30 p.m. with Bimbashi Gastin [French officer with North African troops] on board, also set of Benzine etc (explosives) for Jauf consigned to Abd al Kader for Faisal. Also letters to Abd al Kader and F. Two aeroplanes made flights to north of Mastura, photographs taken. Fired at over Mastura and near Sea, 8 miles north of Rabegh.

25 November. Visited Sharif Ali with Joyce and Ross. Spoke of firing on aeroplanes. Announced arrival of armoured cars and twenty machine guns. Agreed that crews could be trained on beach by Egyptian officers. Khals reported abandoned by Turks. Sharif Ali stated that he adhered to plan of leaving Egyptian troops at Rabegh and had written to Mecca. Did not know what F. intended re. Egyptian troops. Ali [head shaikh of Salim tribe] called in to talk of sending oil and benzine to Jauf. A fine determined man, he had accompanied Faisal to Damascus [in spring of 1916] and when F. returned by train to Hijaz he came to Rabegh overland. He says from here to Jauf would take a loaded camel convoy 20 days. An escort of 50 men would be necessary. Nuri Said spoke privately of differences in pay between Arabs and others. . . . Told him that whole matter was pending settlement of the Aziz al Masri affair. [Aziz had tendered his resignation to the Sharif but he was persuaded to carry on for a few more months.][15]

26 November. Interrogated doctors Tewfiq and Mahmud.

27 November. Flight by aeroplanes to Ibn Hassani and Abu Dhiba.

28 November. HMS *Dufferin* arrived. George Lloyd on board.

29 November. River Fisher arrived. Visited Sharif Ali with Lloyd. Rumour from two Ageyl deserters that Turkish battalion proceeding to Hanakia NE of Madina to check Abdullah had been cut off at Sueidra, a place of twenty wells and many date palms, by Arabs. 45 killed and remainder surrendered. Zaid had written that the Bani Amer had been engaged N. of Khaif and he, Zaid, had heard guns. Turks said to be still at Khals north of Shufia. *Tribal distribution*: Sharif Fahad at Hafa has Bani Jabir, Bani Husain, and Bani Ali; also people of Farai and the Sahman, 600–800 rifles. Shaikh Ali has 1,150 Salima, 500 with rifles, 1,500 Zabeid (70 with rifles), Baladia (200 with rifles) and Humra (80 with rifles). At Hassani there are 1,322 Subh with rifles and some Bani

Salaman. Sharif Ali proposes to send Zaid 1,098 Bishr and Muabbad tribesmen, 750 of whom are without rifles. *Dufferin* left at 2.30 p.m. for Yanbo. G. Lloyd on board.

Telegram to Sirdar, 29 November

Ref. Sirdar's tel. 941 [asking for another appraisal of the Rabegh situation based on a series of questions and confirming Parker's recall to Cairo where Wingate was about to assume the mantle of High Commissioner and General Sir Archibald Murray was about to be replaced by Allenby.] My opinion is as follows:

I assume that the Turkish objective must be Mecca. Leaving the Eastern [mountain] road to the Arabs the only line of advance for the Turks passes through or near Rabegh. The holding of Rabegh therefore appears essential. It seems essential not only against a regular advance but, considering the instability of the Bedouin, against a sudden raid by Camel Corps. Those reasons governed my suggestions for training men at Rabegh after it had been decided not to land British troops. I do not agree that the Turks must destroy a Yanbo force before advancing on Rabegh. I think they could almost ignore it. [The suggestion that Yanbo stood critically in the path of a Turkish advance was Lawrence's theory, put forward in a report on *The Sharif's Position* written while visiting Wingate at Khartoum at the beginning of the month, transmitted by the GOC, Murray, to the DMI London on 17 November.[16] The report also spoke of divided counsels among British advisers.]

I am sure that Aziz al Masri would have got on with Sharif Ali at Rabegh and could have undertaken training here but for Meccan intrigues and the suspicions of the Sharif of Mecca himself. I am not convinced that he will find it easier to work under Faisal than Ali [another Lawrence proposal]. It is inconceivable that he should work directly under us, uncontrolled by the Sharif or his sons.

Rabegh harbour and entrance is infinitely better than Yanbo. The distilling plant at Yanbo can at present turn out 14 tons a day with storage for 50 tons. [water]

Report by OC Flight will follow. An RFC officer yesterday went to Yanbo to report on facilities.

My conception of the situation is that it is first essential to prevent an advance on Mecca and that to ensure this Rabegh should be effectively defended. That done, every concentration of effort should be against the Railway line. I think the reasons for holding Rabegh remain until Turkish power of offensive is gone.

The reasoning which led to the 'trained bands' proposal at Rabegh was that it was deemed necessary to hold Rabegh; the Bedouin could not, and foreign troops were not available. The success of the scheme from the first depended on Aziz having control and obtaining suitable material. Both these factors are now doubtful. I do not think it would be well advised to send Aziz to Sharif unless definite plan first agreed. Plan might be to contract to train a fixed number in specified time for a fixed sum, given entire control and suitable material [recruits]. Objections by Aziz to training at Mecca are that he would be hampered by local intrigues and that force under training would not fulfil functions of Rabegh Defence Forces.

Repeated to Wilson and Arbur.

30 November. Tide very high. Camp on beach nearly submerged. New aeroplane tried. Stores landed, most cases of ground sheets broken open.

River Fisher left for Yanbo 2 p.m. with 59 artillery and 2 Colt guns. Sharif Ali ill but Nuri came to discuss the hardware of Egyptian Battery. It was pointed out that the 'galloping' maxims were of little use in the hills.

1 December. Ships with Indian prisoners arrived 9 a.m. Went aboard and got lists in morning. Met Nuri Bey and took him aboard with other officers to see prisoners. Meetings most cordial in many cases. Much coffee drunk.

2 December. No steamboat [for transport to POW ships] till 9.30 p.m. To ss *Pandua*. Ten [officers] came ashore but after much talk none of them to remain. Afternoon to ss *Kara Deniz* with officers and men (of Arab army) to persuade prisoners. No result. Only one marine officer and a sargeant major willing.

3 December. Began morning with *Kara Deniz* prisoners. Accompanied by Sharif Nasir, Nuri Bey, Rashid Bey and other [Arab] officers. Picked first those who had petitioned in India to join Sharif. All refused. Later five sections seen. All refused. This plan was abandoned and Syrians only were called up in small groups. [Several of these were old friends and co-conspirators of the Arab nationalists in Damascus, but they did not, it seems, like what they saw and heard of the Sharif's army.] All refused. Later single persons were brought in and a few agreed to serve. Having exhausted this means, seven head men were invited to spend the night in the Arab camp on a personal pledge that they would be allowed to return to ship. After some talk they agreed to go.

4 December. Prisoners return to ship. Only one willing to volunteer [for Sharif] and he allowed that he had no following. One or two men were picked out and it was obvious that others would follow only after great delay. Visited *Pandua* and two or three men picked out, and one officer. Others said to be sympathetic to the cause were tried but to no avail. Dined on *Minerva*.

On 5 December Parker handed over as British liaison officer with the Sharifian army to his friend Maj. Joyce. His last act, reflecting perhaps more poignantly than anything else the barren ground he had worked in the first months of the Arab Revolt, was to account for Secret Service funds:

29.10.16	To Haj Abbas. Paid by Hilmi Effendi	.975
30.10.16	To Haj Abbas. Paid by ACP	1.000
30.10.16	Stationery bought on ship	.120
30.10.16	Advance to interpreter, Muhd Amin	5.000
14.11.16	For interpreter's food	3.655
4.12.16	Entertaining Prisoner officers	1.805
	Refunded by ACP to Arbur	7.195
	Handed to Maj. Joyce	380.250
	Taken from chest £400.000	£400.000

[Haj Abbas was Parker's messenger to and from Lawrence at Wadi Safra.]

At 8 a.m. on the 5th he boarded the *Pandua* with the prisoners of war from India who had refused to serve the Sharif, though most of them had expressed support for Arab nationalist aspirations. He occupied himself on the voyage to Suez in writing an account of the protracted interviews with the Moslem prisoners of war, and in composing his final essay to the Arab Bureau.

On the former subject, he wrote: '. . . a pro-Turk Kurd was produced and later a colourless Baghdadi and a Turk from Damascus . . . two Bimbashis of unpleasant type and uncompromising attitude were produced as well as the Adjutant, a young German-speaking Albania educated at the Military School in Constantinople. The beginning did not augur well, nor was it encouraging to hear that the bayonet had been used in Bombay to persuade the officers to leave the train [they had not been told where they were being taken]. One officer received severe wounds in the head and side. The only enthusiastic persons were: an Egyptian journalist who, according to his own account, had been made a prisoner of war at Karachi for no reason and appeared averse to going to Egypt; two doctors, one a Syrian the other Greek, both Christians; and a Kurd who had been an officer in the Police at Baghdad and was looked upon with contempt and distrust by all, including the officers of the Arab army.' Parker repeated the diary details of attempts to introduce the prisoners to Nuri and other Arab officers, aboard the two ships and at camp. He believed that the prisoners were encouraged in their independent attitude by having too much money with them, and he noted: 'A great number of prisoners appeared to be of low Baghdad type and might not have been of much value; nevertheless I think that had the preliminaries been more favourable a useful number of men would have been obtained, the more so had there been a well turned out body of men on the shore with a man of character like Aziz al Masri to inspire confidence and hope for the future.' His report (undated and addressed simply 'Arab Bureau') also observed: 'All the men chosen, however, refused to consider the question at all, and stated that they could not take service against their own Government, the Turks.' He might reasonably have added that had he been writing of British prisoners under duress, their reluctance to engage in an act of treachery would have been found commendable.

Arab Bureau, Cairo, 6 December 1916

On leaving Rabegh it may be well to endeavour to summarise the military situation:

The Turkish offensive, which has always been predicted for the beginning of December, appears about to begin, and they have been reported at Hamra, Wasta, and Bir Said. Aeroplane reconnaissance on 4 December showed numbers of tents in a valley not far north of Hamra, and in one place 113 tents were counted. It is probable that these men were either Turks or pro-Turk Arabs.

Of the Arab forces, Sharif Zaid appears to be retiring on Yanbo, having failed to confront the Turks at Bir Said. Sharif Faisal is at Nakhl Mubarak in the Wadi Yanbo. Sharif Abdullah is somewhere on the Eastern road; and Sharif Ali is at Rabegh.

The latter has already dissipated a considerable part of his force in sending reinforcements to the Yanbo side, having sent to Sharif Zaid and Sharif Faisal at different times about a thousand of his best men as well as two field guns and two mountain guns. If he is shortly to undertake field operations he can ill spare those he has sent. He can certainly spare no more. His outpost at Bir ibn Hassani under Ahmad ibn Mansur is said to have retired on Bir al Shaikh on the arrival of Turks at Wasta. Sharif Ali himself states his intention of advancing in a day or two in the direction of Bir ibn Hassani and has already sent Sharif Shahhab and Sharif Fahad to attack Mijz and Bir al Mashi. It is important that he should advance immediately, since at Rabegh he is fulfilling no useful purpose, nor could he defend Rabegh if it became necessary. The situation for the Arabs seems somewhat critical. The Turks have succeeded in separating the forces of Faisal and Ali and no doubt intend to deal with them one at a time, while comfortably holding off the other. Abdullah may be almost left out of the count, since he is so far away that any offensive action he may take must be merely local attacks made without any idea of co-operation. When the Turks will begin remains to be seen but if they can take possession of the Wadi Yanbo without great difficulty, with all its hamlets and cultivation and no doubt stores of grain, it seems the obvious thing to do, since it will force Faisal father north into less hospitable coutry and necessitate his abandoning Yanbo as a base; and these things, bad enough in themselves, would also be likely to have a very bad effect on the tribes. On the other hand the Turks may be content to hold the passes against Faisal and advance against Ali, hoping that a success in this direction will bring over the tribes, especially those with whom the influence of Husain Mubarak is still good, and so open the road to Mecca. The idea which has been put forward that the hills are impassable cannot be accepted without greater proof of Bedouin co-operation and determination. Where there is passage for a man and a camel a Turkish force can go, nor will it be stopped by snipers only. Husain Mubarak is said to be at Madina and will probably urge Rabegh as the objective, but Wadi Yanbo, if considered feasible, is likely to be undertaken first. One thing which cannot be too much emphasised is that whatever scheme is adopted will probably be German and therefore calculated to damage British interests and prestige.

What the Arabs will do is not easy to say; but it is probable that they will drift along without any combined plan of action, each leader hoping that the other will defeat the Turk. Obviously the necessity of the moment is that Faisal and Ali should in co-operation drive in the posts at Hamra, Wasta and Bir Said, and re-establish communication between their forces. As regards the campaign generally I will make no suggestions except to say that the opinion which I have expressed during the past two months remains my conviction, the more so since the trained bands scheme has failed. The latter was perhaps a somewhat desperate expedient since it depended on the caprice of a most changeable man. Had the Sharif at the first given full trust and authority to Aziz al Masri I believe that a force of some value would have been in existence now, and that such of the Arab prisoners from India as are of any value would have joined it.

The theory has been accepted I am told that the presence of British troops at Rabegh would destroy the Arab tribal spirit. It is a delightful theory and will give pleasure to any Arab enthusiast, but it does not bear clear reasoning. As regards the local situation at Rabegh I suggest that it is most important that the officer in command of the aeroplane escort should have definite and detailed instructions as to what he is expected to do in the event of a Turkish advance, even though such an event is considered improbable. If he is not to make preliminary preparations for an embarkation, for fear of disheartening the Arabs, he must run the risks of losing stores and men. The latter risk must presumably be taken. There is also the question of the two Egyptian Batteries and Company of Infantry at the Arab Camp Rabegh; these are nominally under the command of the Arab leaders, but they look to the British officer commanding the aeroplane escort for instructions in virtue of his position as a senior officer of the Egyptian army. On the departure of the Sharif Ali for the front it would be well to place them directly under the orders of the British Officer Commanding Aeroplane Escort. The Egyptian detachment at Yanbo would also be better moved to Rabegh to join the other Egyptian troops there. From all accounts they are at present ill looked after and inefficient . . .

The report tailed off in topographical and logistical asides.

The Hijaz diary concluded on 7 December. 'Reached Suez 4 p.m. Cairo.'

8
Conclusion

The farcical revolt of the Sharif was to proceed much as before until the armistice was signed at Mudros at the end of October 1918. Wingate officially took over from McMahon on 6 December 1916 and on the 9th Storrs left once more for Jiddah and another abortive meeting with the Sharif. Wilson Pasha, worn down by overwork and worry, asked urgently for Newcombe to be sent down in place of Parker. British authorities in London, Delhi and Cairo began to pay more and more attention to French schemes, suspected and real, in the Arab lands, and to the Sharif's vainglory.

Lawrence, whose chronicle would be for many years the only guide to the War in the Desert, began his seventeenth chapter:

We havered for a while by Yanbo, hoping to retrieve the position: but the tribesmen proved to be useless for assault, and we saw that if the Revolt was to endure we must invent a new plan of campaign at once.

This was hazardous, as the promised British military experts had not yet arrived. However, we decided that to regain the initiative we must ignore the main body of the enemy, and concentrate far off on his railway flank. The first step towards this was to move our base to Wejh: which we proceeded to do in the grand manner.

Newcombe arrived at Yanbo on 18 January 1917 to find a letter from Lawrence dated the 17th waiting for him:

Dear SFN
So I missed you by a day! I'm very sick, but it was either that or miss
Wadi Hamdth again, and that I will certainly see you at Wejh. . . . You'll
find me as good as they say and better . . . .

The promised attack on Rabegh never materialized. The Turks
were content to stay put at Madina; to play cat-and-mouse with
the enemy.

The long-promised attack on Wejh, where a Turkish garrison
held out under the threat of British naval guns, was timed for 23
January. On that day at the appointed time ships under the
command of Capt. Boyle waited for a sign of Faisal's army and its
British adviser who were to have taken the port from the rear.
Some hours after the scheduled time Boyle put a naval and marine
force ashore, and they were led in their assault on the Turkish
HQ, housed in the village school, by Maj. Vickery. Bray was sent
ashore as staff officer to negotiate with the Turks, who held out
bravely until the Royal Navy demolished their temporary citadel.
When the battle was over on the 25th, Faisal and Lawrence
appeared at the head of the desert army.[1] 'A fine sight,' noted
Bray. Twenty-four men from HMS *Fox* had captured fifty-five
Turks and killed twelve. They suffered one loss, Lieut. Stewart.

Lawrence explained later that he and Faisal had been held up
for lack of water. Then came the taking of Aqaba and finally the
rush to Damascus, to gain a foothold in the Syrian capital before
Allenby's men, and more particularly the French, could estabish
themselves.[2] Throughout the two years of the Arab Revolt, the
Turkish force at Madina under the command of Fakhri Pasha the
amiable old butcher of the Armenians, and the Maan force under
Jamal II (Kuchuk) held out against numerically superior Arab
armies; and despite the brave and prodigious efforts of Garland
and his Arabs, and later of Newcombe and Lawrence, the railway
from Damascus to Madina remained operational over its 900-
mile track with only minor interruptions. Looking back over the
course of that famous 'side show', truthful military observers

would say that the real achievement belonged not to Britain and its Arab allies but to the Turks; that for two more years the Sharifians danced to Fakhri's tune.

Parker resumed control of the Sinai Peninsula early in 1917, returning to the fortress of Al Arish where a eucalyptus grove he had planted before the war was now in the fulness of youth. Allenby had moved up his GHQ by now and Wallier was given an office in the old castle that had once been his home. But he was happy to combine the roles of Military Governor and General Staff Officer under the dynamic command of the new C-in-C, the man who in France had acquired the nickname 'the Bull'.

McMahon's final official act was to send to the Foreign Secretary for onward transmission to the people concerned a record of his appreciation of the help he had received from members of the Arab Bureau – Aubrey Herbert, George Lloyd, Gertrude Bell, T. E. Lawrence, Clayton, Hogarth, Fforde (the reluctant representative of the Indian Government) and last but not least, Parker:

The High Commissioner's message to the Foreign Office, dated 20 December 1916, included the paragraph:

Lt. Colonel A. C. Parker superintended the work of the Bureau during the absence in England of Brigadier-General Clayton in June and July 1916. Subsequently he was detailed by the Commander-in-Chief, Egyptian Expeditionary Force, as Liaison Officer with the Arab forces at Rabegh, where his knowledge and experience of Arabs was of great assistance.

On 7 December 1916, Parker was officially listed as Military Governor of Sinai. But his actual return to pre-war pastures was delayed. He was required to serve jointly on the new C-in-C's staff at Al Arish, and to move up with the army as it pursued the Turks through Palestine. His great knowledge of the Arabs and his ability to converse with the Bedouin made him invaluable to Allenby, and he was to become Governor of Arish until the end of the war, temporary Governor of Jaffa (an appointment which lasted only a few days), as a General Staff Officer Grade 1, along with his responsibility for Sinai. The diary from January 1917 marks his progress and his meetings with Arabs and Jews as the 'Bull' rolled up the Ottoman carpet. But there is none of the detail which accompanied his Hijaz sojourn. By the autumn of 1917 army GHQ had moved to Um al Kalab near the border village of Rafa. The Expeditionary Force had hauled with it a railway track and a water tapline through the fiery heat. One of Parker's tasks now was to maintain contact with agents in Palestine, Syria and Sinai, with the invaluable help of Issairi, and other friendly shaikhs of old acquaintance among the Arabs of the Peninsula. His immediate chief was Guy Dawnay, deputy to Allenby's Chief of Staff Maj.-Gen. Sir Louis Bols. The diary gives tantalizingly meagre glimpses of the staff's work as the army moved on towards Jerusalem and up through the Plain of Philistia.

Allenby had brought his own intelligence chief to Cairo, Col. Richard Meinertzhagen, a laughing man of great size and strength, matching the 'Bull' in physique and force of personality. And from the first Meinertzhagen had employed as his principal agent the brilliant Zionist Aaron Aaronsohn whose agricultural research station at Athlit near Haifa had been turned into the most important spy station in Palestine. Aaron was then in Cairo, and the Palestinian spy ring was controlled by his sister Sarah. From November 1915, contact had been made between GHQ and Athlit by the monitor and spy ships of the navy. But this method of obtaining information and dropping agents had become increasingly difficult despite Allenby's successful advance.

One of the little ships, Lord Rosebery's pre-war yacht *Zaida* which had been taken over by Leonard Woolley the intelligence chief at Port Said, had been sunk in 1916 while its new owner was joy-riding off Alexandretta. Woolley had been taken prisoner by the Turks. Parker's Sinai conveyance HMY *Managam* had taken over, with occasional help from the *Anne* (when seaplanes were needed). By 1917 the Germans had established an effective spy base around Haifa and Jaffa, organized by Herr Kurt Wagner, one of the remarkable group that had travelled from Berlin to Afghanistan in the early days of 1915 to promote holy war on the North-West Frontier, and who had returned through Asia Minor

against all the odds to continue their work in Syria. One of
Parker's final tasks in the campaign was to arrest Wagner. The
Turks had several times sighted the *Managam* as it lay off shore at
dusk, receiving signals from the Jewish spies at Athlit, and
submarines now patrolled the coastal waters. And so in August
1917, GHQ at Um Kalab organized a pigeon messenger service
under Col. Parker's control. Late in September one of the birds
decided to feed in the garden of one of Jamal Pasha's mudirs. It
was caught and the coded message attached to it resulted in an
intensive search for the spy ring which was known to be operating
close to Haifa. On 1 October Jamal's gendarmes descended on the
Aaronsohn home at Zichron Yakov and arrested Sarah and
several of her companions. Sarah committed suicide by shooting
herself through the mouth after four days of torture. Other
members of the ring were rounded up and hanged. By then they
had done their work and Allenby's army was at the gates of Jaffa
and Jerusalem.

The diary, resuming in August, tells only of assignations;
nothing of the dramatic events during this period. Such things are
not committed to paper in the heat of battle. There are long
gaps, and occasional reports, on the liberated zones, or occupied
enemy territory.

1 August 1917. Worked at prisoners in compound.

2 August. Intelligence urgently asked to supply own man at Kanṭara.

3 August. Issairi Eff. to Rafa to drive Arabs south of their line. Rode to
Shaikh Zowaid. Trained to Arish.

4 August. Quarantine restrictions re-imposed.

5 August. Rode to beach to inspect rest camp buildings . . . certain to be
destroyed by sea in winter. Saw Tih shaikhs. Also Shahada. In morning
saw General Watson (Commander Northern Force). Discussed impossibility of working present Intelligence system. Interference. Removal of
wireless from Al Arish.

6 August. With General Watson to Khan Yunis [PoW camp]. Considered proposals of Intelligence for tightening cordon etc.

7 August. Heard case of escape of Barak Ayada.

8 August. Visited Abu Sajal.

9–18 August. Al Arish. Met Allenby to discuss 'quails and dates'. Saw Gen. Kitson. Examined persons under detention.

26 August. Rode to Shaikh Zowaid.

5–21 September. Shaikh Zowaid and Al Arish. On 21st meeting of Municipal Council, Arish. Two Australians drunk in town.

4–5 October. GHQ with Gilbert Clayton.

7–9 October. Heavy rain. 9th. Wagner arrested and premises searched (on Jaffa road). Arrangements for location of Jammas [?] south of Jaffa in sand hills.

11 October. Wire. Return to GHQ.

30 October. Rode to Khan Yunis. Discussed offices for OET. [He was now much concerned with restoring services and supplies in the towns which had been left without administration by the withdrawal of the Turks. The diary contains lists of supplies required by villagers, as well as requests such as 'He asked that the tomb of Sayidna Khidr might be repaired.']

1 November. Rode round Bir al Saba. [Beersheba had fallen on 31 October and the Deputy Ajutant-General had asked Parker to arrange for Gen. Malcolm to go there with one of his Arab officers, Fuad Effendi and a party of Sudanese rifles.][3]

2 November. GHQ. Obtained copy of C-in-C's Proclamation. [The Proclamation was to be read at the taking of Jerusalem, which did not fall until December.]

3 November. DAG visited Beersheba and was rather worried by numbers of Arabs in the place looting. MacCallum [Brig.-Gen.] asked me to go there next day.

4 November. Breakfast No. 1 mess GHQ. Left by motor for Beersheba at 8.10 with Col. Wemyss. Arrived 10.10. Things getting straight. Arabs being dealt with.

7 November. Sheria and Harera taken by army.

8 November. Gaza taken.

12 November. To Gaza by car. Destruction and desolation.

13 November. GHQ with Gen. Watson. Talking all morning.

14 November. Abdal Hadi and Ibrahim al Hussaini [of a family destined to play an important part in Palestine affairs, many of whom had served in the Turkish army].

15 November. GHQ. Talk of Police.

16 November. Evans turned up [Maj.-Gen. Sir Edward Evans, Allenby's chief of administration, presently trying to re-organize tax collection].

19 November. To Jaffa by car with Issairi via Richon la Zion. [Jaffa had fallen to Allenby on 16 November.]

20 November. Jaffa.

Within a few hours of his arrival Parker compiled a detailed report for the DAG.

DAG. GHQ Jaffa 20.11.17
I arrived here last night and after a day's examination my estimate is as follows:
[There is a long appraisal of measures taken or to be taken regarding the

collection of arms, registration, reporting of enemy subjects, work required on roads and buildings, the availability of ships, steam-rollers, horses etc, and then an account of the state of the town and its Jewish quarter of Tel Aviv.]

(6) Of the normal population of 65,000, the Turks had removed all but 2,000. Since the British occupation refugees have been returning and the numbers in the town may be from 8-10,000. Perhaps another 10,000 will return. There is some distress among the poorer classes and this will tend to increase at first. Prices are high and foodstuffs are scarce.

(7) A number of needy persons, chiefly children, are being cared for at the CMS Hospital by French Sisters of St Joseph. Two hundred of the poor were sometime ago sent to Jerusalem and thence to Bethlehem leaving 144 at present in the CMS Hospital at Jaffa. The relief is carried out under a committee of Towns' folk and was supported in Turkish times by forced donations. They have some supplies but chiefly of millet. The ration is inadequate and the children look wan and in some cases emaciated. Clothing, bedding, mattresses and money are urgently needed. As a temporary measure I have ordered an increase in the ration and the addition of fresh meat and vegetables. If the CMS will take it in hand, I suggest they be urged to move quickly and given transport by HM Navy. They should anticipate considerably more than the 144 mentioned and be prepared to give outdoor relief in addition if they will. I cannot estimate the stocks in the town, but it would be as well to bring 20 tons of wheat flour with them.

(8) It has been represented by the townsfolk that general bankruptcy and distress will ensue unless a rate for paper money is fixed. I think they exaggerate, and at an estimate there is probably not more than £20,000 worth of notes held in the town. Things will necessarily be difficult until Egyptian and British coinage begin to be plentiful.

(9) The orange crop is estimated at 300,000 boxes this year and means for moving it to a market, if not to England at least to Egypt, are earnestly sought by the townspeople. Wood is available for about 30,000 boxes, but no nails. The people request that sailing boats be permitted to ply between Jaffa and Port Said and Alexandria. This I urge should be considered. The time for orange shipments is from now on for the next four months.

(10) Arrangements are being made to collect Mukhtars (admin.

officials) of villages and obtain control through them. My estimate of the conditions of villagers is that they have seed grain and food, and that they will bring more grain to the town market as soon as the rains ensure the next harvest. In Turkish times these fellahin (peasant cultivators) generally refused to accept paper money and, though very heavily taxed, received a greatly enhanced price for whatever they sold.

(11) A list is being prepared of Turkish Government employees in Jaffa . . . Also Police.

(12) The three banks are all closed and everything is said to have been removed to Jerusalem: Deutsche Palestina Bank, Ottoman Bank, Anglo-Palestine Bank. The establishment of a banking institution to assist in restoring conditions will be essential.

(13) I have not yet examined the cases of German and other enemy residents. They report daily to the Military Commandant. In the case of the proprietor of the only hotel – at surface value it is not desirable that a German of long connection in the neighbourhood should be in close touch with British officers. The hotel is in running order and of value to keep open. I suggest that a British or other Company purchase the property and run it.

(14) The municipal council, whose income is said to be £7000 per annum, is at present in operation. I am therefore engaging sweepers etc.

(15) I require £500 in small silver, at the first available opportunity.

(16) The key to solving all the troubles of Jaffa and its distress, is the opening of some door for the placing of its oranges on the market. Automatically everyone will receive pay and employment.

That sociological essay on the Palestinian town which Jamal had emptied in March 1917 when the Turks repulsed the latest British attack on Gaza, was his last report from the front line. The diary for 1917 concludes with notes of meetings and administrative affairs:

22 November. To GHQ [now at Bir Salem, between Jaffa and Jerusalem], to meet General Adye [Maj.-Gen. Commander Southern Force]. He did not arrive. Flag removed.

23 November. GHQ with Gen. Clayton [now Chief Political Officer, Palestine] and Jellicoe.

27 November. Jewish Zionists visit me.

27 November. Jewish Colonists visit me. Air raid, 9 killed and 16 wounded. Germans sent off with Anzacs. Archimandrite arrested and released.

1 December. Gen. Clayton and M. Picot called. Met Col. Deedes (political intelligence chief) and Meinertzhagen (DMI). Discussed clearing of zone.

By now Sinai had been cleared of the enemy and Wallier Parker was asked to resume his old job as Governor of his beloved wasteland. He remained there as undisputed ruler and the friend of the Arab tribes, until 1923, and forever after the people of Sinai would remember Parker Pasha or as they would have it still 'Birkil'. The relationship with the tribes established in pre-war days, paternalistic and always even-handed, resumed as though the intervening years of conflict and taking of sides had not happened. When he returned to Nakhl in May 1918, Allenby wrote him a personal note:

My dear Parker
I have just got your letter of 27th. I'm sorry I missed seeing you before you went, as I wanted to thank you for all the good work you have done while with me. I am most grateful to you, and am sorry to lose you. With all good wishes,

Ever yours,
Edmund Allenby

When the Sultan Fuad of Egypt was crowned King in 1922, following the Declaration of Independence for which Allenby had pressed almost from the moment of his appointment as High Commissioner for Egypt in succession to Wingate in March 1919, Parker was asked to collect together the tribal leaders of Sinai and

29. V. 18

My dear Parker,

I have just got your letter of 27. —

I'm sorry I missed seeing you before you went, as I wanted to thank you for all the good work you have

Letter from General Allenby to Parker on the latter's return to Sinai, May 1918

read to them the royal proclamation. The sons of Ishmael listened with due solemnity. They guessed from Birkil's tone that his message was important. When he had finished the shaikhs rushed forward with outstretched arms, shouting *Mubarak! Mubarak!* Congratulations![4]

They thought that he was announcing his own coronation as King of Egypt. In 1924, succeeded by Claude Jarvis, he was made Director-General of the Frontier Districts Administration. But by the end of that year he and almost all the other British advisers left behind in that Egypt of equivocal independence, resigned. On 19 November Sir Lee Oliver Stack, who had succeeded Wingate as Sirdar and Governor-General of the Sudan in 1917, was shot when leaving the War Ministry in Cairo. He died the next day in the British Residency. As the mortally injured Stack, the ex-intelligence chief, was carried into the Residency, a dinner party was interrupted at which former Prime Minister Asquith was the principal guest. After dinner the Egyptian nationalist leader Zaghul arrived. Allenby had supported his claims and released him from imprisonment, despite strong opposition from the home government. Allenby turned angrily on his protégé and told him 'This is your doing'. But the real culprits, though known to the authorities, were never arrested and the British resigned *en bloc*.

Parker had been awarded the Egyptian Order of the Nile in 1917, the DSO in 1918, and the Legion of Honour in the same year. He retired to the family home at Minchinhampton in Gloucestershire and seldom spoke of his wartime adventures or friendships. He came out of his seclusion once, in November 1927, to talk to the Central Asian Society (the Royal Society for Asian Affairs as it was to become), and in the audience were several of his war comrades and his senior officer in Intelligence, Gen. Sir Gilbert Clayton. Field-Marshal Viscount Allenby took the chair.

Clayton recalled that, up to the beginning of the war, the administration of Sinai was vested in the Intelligence Department of the Egyptian War Office, and was not under the Ministry of the

Interior. 'It was under that department,' he observed, 'that Colonel Parker worked when he first went to Sinai.' 'Bertie' went on to talk of some of the feats of the Intelligence Department and of Parker Pasha, or as the Arabs called him to the end 'Birkil Beq'.

Allenby said: 'I have known him for a good many years. I met him at his headquarters at Al Arish in the early days of the Palestinian campaign, and saw him then among what I will call his subjects of Mount Sinai. I saw the respect, almost amounting to veneration, which he commanded.'

He died, as he had lived and worked, steadfast and uncomplaining, on 27 December 1935, at the age of sixty-one.

When news of his death reached Col. Davenport – the soldier to whom, as Lawrence had said, the Arabs owed their greatest foreign debt – he called together a group of Arab campaigners to compose a joint tribute which *The Times* published on 3 January 1936. After listing his career details, they wrote:

Among his fellow countrymen he will long be remembered as 'Sinai Parker'. . . . His knowledge of Arabic was profound. In his dealings with the Beduin that motionless face and steady gaze would puzzle them, and, wondering in their perplexity what he really knew, they would blurt out the truth. His kindly knowledge of human nature won him their love and affection and the name of 'Birkil' was one to conjure with in the peninsula. Before Parker's administration of Sinai, only primitive Arab law existed. It was the law of retribution, 'an eye for an eye, a a tooth for a tooth'. Parker was largely responsible for getting the Sinai law framed and promulgated in 1911. In 1915 he conducted a completely successful minor expedition against a Turco-Arab force which was threatening. . . Tor, in southern Sinai. . . . . Later his intimate knowledge of the country and people made him an invaluable link between the British forces and the Beduin. . . . The best of companions, a wise counsellor, and a sterling friend.

Notes

Chapter 1: Baptism in Sinai (pp. 21–40)

1. Towara, plural of Tor; Arabs of the peninsula south of Jabal Tih.

2. In a lecture to the Central Asian Society on 2 November, 1927, Col. Parker stated: 'I first made acquaintance with the peninsula in 1906 at the time of what is called 'The Aqaba Incident'. Disagreements had arisen as to the boundary between Sinai, as part of Egypt, and Turkey, there being no delimitated line. It was then reported that the only definite boundary mark, two old pillars under a tree at Rafa on the Mediterranean, were being removed by the Turks . . . I was sent to Al Arish. My next visit to Sinai was to a very different scene. The Aqaba incident was pursuing its course of diplomatic discussion, and to strengthen the Egyptian arguments HMS *Diana* was sent to Aqaba, and a detachment of Egyptian infantry to Farun Island, near the head of the Gulf. . . . An agreement was eventually come to with the Turks, and arrangements made for a delimitation Commission, which later on moved over the country between Aqaba and Rafa, and fixed on a line. It fell to my lot to arrange the building of the pillars (150, I think) marking the line . . . By this time I was in charge of the whole peninsula, with head-quarters at Nakhl, eighty miles east of Suez.' The Turkish landing was in fact at Taba, the actual frontier post . The landing was closely followed by the Dinshawi Incident, resulting in the resignation of Cromer.

3. Greek inscription in Wadi Mukkatab, G. Murray, *Sons of Ishmael*,

Routledge, 1935, p. 256n.

4. Col. Charles Warren, a staff officer with the Egyptian expeditionary force and Capt. Sir Richard Burton, Consul at Trieste, were sent to Sinai to track down the murderers. Warren, later Commissioner of London's police force, ran most of them to ground. The extent to which the true purpose of the mission was kept from the public is revealed by H. J. L. Beadnell writing in 1927 (*The Wilderness of Sinai*): Palmer and companions were 'purchasing camels for Wolseley's force'. Kitchener, then a major surveying Palestine for the War Office, was told: Arabi sent to Governor of Nakhl a message that he had utterly destroyed all Christian ships of war at Alexandria and Suez. 'If Christians found in Sinai – like rats with no holes – to be killed at once.' A. Mary R. Dobson, *Mount Sinai*, Methuen, 1925. See also Walter Besant, *The Life and Achievements of Edward Henry Palmer*, Murray, 1883.

5. Place or building containing spirit of departed.

6. Palestine Exploration Fund, Quarterly Statement, 1880, p. 158.

7. *Desert of the Exodus*, Bell & Dalby, 1871.

8. Murray, op. cit., p. 245.

9. There are two buildings at the summit of Jabal Musa, the chapel of Moses and a Moslem mosque supposedly built over the cave where Moses lived during the forty days and nights of vision. According to Burckhardt, *Travels in Syria*, Arabs still believed that rainfall in Sinai was controlled by Moses, and that the Convent possessed the *Turat*, a book received by Moses from heaven. Two other convents are situated in the valley which runs at the foot of Mount Sinai (Jabal Musa); the Convent of the Forty Martyrs, and the Convent of the Twelve Apostles.

The first monks and hermits settled at Feiran, 25 miles north-west of Jabal Musa, at the beginning of the Christian era. Many lost their lives at the hands of the Badu. Helena, the mother of Constantine, learnt of the plight of the monks during a visit to Jerusalem in AD 327 and caused the building of a tower of refuge at the foot of the mountain which became the Monastery of St Catherine. Napoleon was instrumental in saving the building from collapse during the Egyptian campaign at the end of the eighteenth century. In 1859 the German theologian Constantine von Tischendorf discovered the famous *Codex Sinaiticus*, the parchment manuscript of the Bible, in the monastery. It was purchased by the Czar of Russia from the monks for 9,000 roubles. It subsequently found its way to the Library of St Petersburg, and finally to the British Museum which bought it from the Soviet Government in 1933 for £100,000. See Werner, Keller, *The Bible as History*, Hodder & Stoughton (1956).

10. Parker estimated population of al Arish as 7,000, Tor 1,200 and entire peninsula 20–25,000.

11. C.S. Jarvis, *Three Deserts*, Murray, 1936.

12. Sir Osbert Sitwell, *Great Morning*, p. 26.

13. W. M. Flinders Petrie, *Researches in Sinai*, Murray, 1906, p. 53.

14. Parker, Lecture to Central Asian Society, 2 November 1927.

15. Murray, op. cit., p. 58.

Chapter 2: The Threads of War (pp. 41–52)

1. Col. A. Jennings Bramly officially succeeded Parker at Nakhl, but from this time on it was thought impolitic to maintain a British governor on the spot. Barlow was designated, Nazir (police chief) and Bramly spent most of his time with the Survey of Egypt in Cairo.

2. See Winstone, *The Illicit Adventure*, Cape, 1982.

Chapter 3: War in Sinai (pp. 53–82)

1. Not until the end of 1915 when the evacuation of the Dardanelles was mooted, was a senior GS officer appointed – Brig.-Gen. Neil Malcolm. Holdich was graded GSO3.

2. Kreiss von Kressenstein, *Sinai*, pp. 2–18.

3. Mission led by Oberstleutenant von Niedermayer, the Political Agent Wassmuss and diplomat Von Hentig, angrily disposed to one another. Hundreds of men, guns and animals were involved.

4. See L. B. Weldon, *Hard Lying*, Jenkins, 1925.

5. Official History of the War, *Egypt and Palestine*, MacMunn & Falls, p. 28.

6. Enseigne de Vasseau Potier de la Morandiere, quoted in Official History.

7. The military significance of Tor was its command of the Gulf of Suez, of course.

8. Letter postmarked Near Suez, 27 March 1915 from Capt. Salter to

Mother and Father and Sister Olive. Courtesy Mrs. D. St C. Candler.

   9. WO 33/796. Haldane to GOC.

   10. Murray, op. cit., 144-5.

Chapter 4: General Staff, Cairo (pp. 83–107)

   1. For description of the intrigues of the European powers and movements of British agents – T. E. Lawrence, Leonard Woolley, Gertrude Bell and Capt. Shakespear – see the author's *The Illicit Adventure*. Also *Arabian Studies*, VI, p. 214 (Middle East Centre, Cambridge), in which Dr Robin Bidwell suggests the possibility that at this time Lawrence and Faisal bin Husain, the Prince of Mecca, may have been members of the clandestine Damascus Committee (quoting records of the Service Historique de l'Armee Vincennes, Adjutant Lamotte, 9 May 1917, Box 7N 2141). See also Jacques Benoist-Mechin, *Arabian Destiny*, Elek, 1957, pp. 112–15, visit of delegates of al-Fattah (civil wing of Damascus Committee), to Ibn Saud to seek his support and leadership.

   2. Official History, p. 54.

   3. Murray, op. cit., p. 51.

   4. H. A. Macmichael was a civilian working for the Survey of India Department and seconded to Staff Intelligence. He was the author of *A History of the Arabs in the Sudan*, Cambridge, 1922.

   5. Bidwell, op. cit., p. 186.

   6. Murray, op. cit., p. 247.

   7. Ibn Hadhal was 'bought' by Leachman in 1916 and was a loyal ally of Britain during the war. Nuri Shalan, despite Lawrence's sympathetic account in *Seven Pillars of Wisdom*, (Penguin, 1962) remained faithful to the Turks until the last days of the war.

   8. This was again inaccurate. Musil, who was present, describes taking of Jauf by Nuri's son Nawaf, who presented it to his father. But Nuri did not go to his capital for several months after its capture.

   9. See Bidwell, op. cit., p. 213.

   10. For destruction of Syrian nationalist movement, see *Arab Bulletin*, no. 1, 6 May 1916.

   11. Gen. Sir J. Wolfe Murray.

Chapter 5: The Arab Bureau (pp. 109–113)

1. K. to Abdullah, 24 September 1914, FO882.
2. See Winstone, op. cit. Chapter 9.
3. A name omitted by both Lawrence and Hogarth was Capt. the Hon. W. A. ('Billy') Ormsby-Gore.

Chapter 6: The Desert War (pp. 115–146)

1. Sir Gilbert Clayton, *An Arabian Diary*, ed. by Robert O. Collins, University of California Press, 1969, pp. 66-7.
2. WO 33/820.
3. Although the Sharif refused to permit Britain or its allies to use agents inside his territory, news reached the War Office of events from the declaration of the Revolt in early June until Parker's arrival in September was mainly derived from radio interception in Cairo of German and Turkish coded messages, and from the signals of Capt. Boyle the SNO in the Red Sea.

The small Turkish garrison at Mecca (most of the force having gone to the hill station of Taif for the hot season), surrendered on 12 June when a numerically superior Arab force set fire to the barracks. Two small forts in the holy city held out, however, for several weeks until heavy guns were brought from Jiddah to compel their surrender. An Arab force of some 30,000 under Sharif Ali attacked Madina on 6 June, but was severely defeated; Ali then marched on the railway near Medain Saleh, 180 miles to the north-west, but was driven off. On 9 June, 4,000 Arabs of the Bani Harb attacked Jiddah but were beaten off by a garrison with artillery and machine-guns. On 11 June the port was bombarded by the converted India Marine ship *Hardinge* and the light cruiser *Fox*, while planes from the *Ben-my-Chree* dropped bombs on several targets. On 16th the Turkish force 1,400 men, 45 officers and 16 guns surrendered. The 3,000 Turks at Taif, armed with ten 75-mm Krupp guns, held out against Abdullah's superior Arab force until September, and was still resisting under siege when Parker left for the Red Sea. The entire Turkish force in western Arabia was estimated by Britain's War Office at 15,000, mainly the 22nd Division under Fakhri at Madina and the 21st, based in Asir, with battalions at Lith and Qunfidah on the Hijaz coast. Allied strategy from the outset was to immobilize the Hijaz railway, while using the Royal Navy to control the coastline. But this demanded the support of the Billi tribe which commanded much of the railroad, with the Howaitat farther north. The Shaikh of the Billi, Suleiman Pasha, was uncooperative however.

By July, the German mission lead by Major Othmar von Stotzingen with the approval of Faisal (who was with Jamal in Damascus until late May), had been betrayed by shaikhs of the Harb tribe and had withdrawn hurriedly to Damascus. A force of 3,500 specially picked men under Col. Khairi Bey which accompanied them had joined Fakhri in Madina. Another German party of nine men under Lt. von Muecke was attacked by Arabs led by one of Jaussen's agents, a Harbi pirate named Auda ibn Zubaida, and most were murdered. Stotzingen and his companions joined the second assault on Suez which took place in July.

4. Wingate took charge of all military affairs in the Hijaz in June. WO 33/728.

5. Lawrence, op. cit., p. 95.

6. Also refers to holy carpet traditionally brought from Egypt.

7. Ali Haider Pasha, of rival house of Ashraf (nobles), nominated by Porte as Naqib al-Ashraf and Sharif of Mecca on proclamation of Revolt. He was married to an Irish woman and his eldest son was educated in England. He arrived at Madina on 26 July. A statement issued by the Ottoman Legation at Berne on 2 September asserted that, as British warships had bombarded the Turkish garrison at Jidah on 11 June, the Sharif had telegraphed the Porte telling the Imperial Government that he awaited confirmation of title 'Sharif' being made hereditary within his family, in which case he would place himself at the disposal of the Government and send a detachment to assist in second attack on Suez.

8. Bidwell, op. cit., Box 7N 2139, SHA, Vincennes.

9. WO 33/738, secret tels. Mediterranean.

10. See Lawrence, op. cit., pp. 309–20.

11. Official History , p. 54.

12. WO 33/820.

13. WO 33/905.

14 The subject of combat troops from non-Islamic countries fighting in the Hijaz was complicated by the Sharif's inability to make up his mind, and by the fears of the British Government. Eventually Col.

Wilson asked the Sharif to demand British troops for Rabegh in writing, but he refused. Official History, p. 234.

15. FO 371/2776.

16. WO 33/728.

17. The Sirdar, an administrative fuss-pot, was known to all and sundry in Egypt and the Sudan as 'Master'. See Clayton, op. cit.

18. Arrived 10 September with Indian Moslem soldiers for Hajj, see Bray, op. cit.

19. FO 371/2776 and FO 882/5.

20. CAB 42/21.

21. Sykes-Picot, 16 May 1916.

22. FO 882/5.

23. FO 371/2776.

24. Sir Ronald Storrs, *Orientations*.

Chapter 7: The New Regime (pp. 147–186)

1. WO 33/905.

2. Bidwell, Arabian Studies III, and Bray, *Shifting Sands*, Unicorn, 1934.

3. FO 372/832.

4. See Clayton, *An Arabian Diary*, pp. 66–8.

5. Reference presumably to invasion by Muhammad Ali's army in 1811–18.

6. Storrs, op. cit.

7. Map references from WO 4011 using letters of place-names for Parker's guidance.

8. Note from T. E. Lawrence dated 23rd.

9. FO 371/2776.

10. L/P&S/10/387.

11. See Winstone, op. cit., ch. 12.

12. 12. FO 371/2776.

13. CAB 42/19 and 42/24.

14. Lawrence, op. cit., p. 112.

15. Retired September 1917, see Winstone, op. cit., note to p. 320.

16. WO 33/728.

Chapter 8: Conclusion (pp. 187–199)

1. 'A serious lack of initiative,' Winstone, op. cit., p. 256.

2. See Winstone, op. cit., p. 331 and notes.

3. One of the most heroic exploits in the taking of Beersheba and opening the road to Jerusalem was that of Col. Newcombe who had returned to Egypt in July after being injured in an attack on the Hijaz railroad. He led seventy men on camels in a diversionary attack, and was taken prisoner.

4. Report of RSAA meeting, November 1927.

General Index

Index to Places